Customer Relationship Management

T0341558

MARKETING

04.04

Michael J. Cunningham

- Fast track route to developing world class customer relationships

- Covers all the key techniques for successful customer relationship management, from developing profitable customer relationships to integrated sales management systems and from e-marketing to pricing

- Examples and lessons from some of the world's most successful businesses, including Cisco and EclipsysEMC, and ideas from the smartest thinkers, including Don Peppers, Thomas Siebel and Patricia Seybold

- Includes a glossary of key concepts and a comprehensive resources guide

>> EXPRESS EXEC . COM <<
essential management thinking at your fingertips

The right of Michael J. Cunningham to be identified as the author of this work
has been asserted in accordance with the Copyright, Designs and Patents Act
1988

First published 2002 by
Capstone Publishing (a Wiley company)
8 Newtec Place
Magdalen Road
Oxford OX4 1RE
United Kingdom
http://www.capstoneideas.com

CIP catalogue records for this book are available from the British Library and the
US Library of Congress

ISBN 1-84112-213-0

This book is printed on acid-free paper

Substantial discounts on bulk quantities of Capstone books are available
to corporations, professional associations and other organizations. Please
contact Capstone for more details on +44 (0)1865 798 623 or (fax) +44
(0)1865 240 941 or (e-mail) info@wiley-capstone.co.uk

FSC

Mixed Sources
Product group from well-managed
forests and other controlled sources

Cert no. SGS-COC-2953
www.fsc.org
© 1996 Forest Stewardship Council

Contents

Introduction to ExpressExec

ExpressExec is 3 million words of the latest management thinking compiled into 10 modules. Each module contains 10 individual titles forming a comprehensive resource of current business practice written by leading practitioners in their field. From brand management to balanced scorecard, ExpressExec enables you to grasp the key concepts behind each subject and implement the theory immediately. Each of the 100 titles is available in print and electronic formats.

Through the ExpressExec.com Website you will discover that you can access the complete resource in a number of ways:

» printed books or e-books;
» e-content – PDF or XML (for licensed syndication) adding value to an intranet or Internet site;
» a corporate e-learning/knowledge management solution providing a cost-effective platform for developing skills and sharing knowledge within an organization;
» bespoke delivery – tailored solutions to solve your need.

Why not visit www.expressexec.com and register for free key management briefings, a monthly newsletter and interactive skills checklists. Share your ideas about ExpressExec and your thoughts about business today.

Please contact elound@wiley-capstone.co.uk for more information.

Introduction to Customer Relationship Management

What is the role of CRM in the modern world of business? This chapter considers the changing nature of CRM, including:

» why companies need to user Customer Relationship Management as a competitive weapon;
» despite a high failure rate, why many companies continue to implement CRM solutions.

Few topics in the New Economy have aroused such considerable discussion and trepidation as the issue of Customer Relationship Management (CRM). One of the amazing facts about CRM is that, despite a failure rate of close to 60% in the systems that are developed, companies and organizations still continue to buy it in droves. Why, if the technology and the implementation fail at this rate – more than 20% higher than industry norms for enterprise-wide IT systems – would they continue to try and implement the systems? The reason is that ones that work, work really well, and CRM is a technology that no organization can do without.

CRM is not a new technology, but the way that it can be used in today's environment can be very different. CRM has evolved from the base of many systems, where the functions were initially defined at the department level, and gradually moved up to the enterprise. Organizations keep the information about their client base inside the organizations, but not necessarily accessible to the other parts of the operation or capable of being leveraged by them. For this reason much of the information about clients and how we work with them is very fragmented.

Finance has customer information, Customer Support has another database, Sales might be using sales force automation systems or a simple contact manager. Desktops in the office may use Outlook, and marketing departments have their own databases. In each case, the information that is available may be complete up to a point, but is unlikely to be comprehensive. As many organizations have tried to solve their customer relationship problems using technology overlaid on existing work processes, many of the failures are a result of poor productivity gains. If an electronic system merely overlays an existing, and perhaps inefficient, process, then at best the improvement is zero, and often lower than this, because of the additional maintenance and administration of these systems.

IMPROVING BUSINESS OPERATIONS – RETURN ON INVESTMENT

Most organizations are ready to spend money on this area. After all, when you have a worldwide market of $23bn in products and services,[1] rising to an expected $76.3bn in 2003, someone is spending a lot of money. The primary goal today has to be in the area of spending this money and gaining successful outcomes for the organization. The failure rates cannot remain at this astonishing level. This book will focus on what has worked for organizations that have successfully figured out what this subject really means to them, and translated it into measurable Return on Investment or business improvements that cause them to use CRM as a weapon in business, not just a tool.

As with most technologies, CRM is not an elixir to be taken alone. Successful systems are a careful blend of technology, work process change, and metrics to support the business goals intended to be affected by the use of the systems. While the technology field for this area can be confusing, there are ways of ensuring that improvements are measured effectively. This book will provide directions for this roadmap and help you attain satisfactory results in the development of your systems.

NOTE

1 Source: Gartner Group.

Definition of Terms

Many do not even know what the acronym CRM stands for, but they understand the value of leveraging customer relationships. Building a CRM solution is more difficult. This chapter examines some of the classic definitions of brand. It includes:

» what is CRM and how to take advantage of it;
» who owns CRM inside the organization;
» what CRM applications are typically implemented;
» the CRM financial payoff;
» the customer revolution (Patricia Seybold).

WHAT IS CRM?

Customer Relationship Management is a term defined to describe how we interact and proactively manage our *Customer Relationships*. It is particularly important to understand that CRM is really a system in the truest sense – the system of how we work with our customers, solve problems for them, encourage them to purchase products and services, and deal with the financial transactions. In a nutshell, it includes all aspects of our interactions with clients.

It is all of the elements inside the business associated with the customer function connected in an intelligent manner. Customer management processes, supported by the business rules of the operation and technology making it all hang together. CRM can be complex because of the nature of business. Much of the day-to-day aspects of business are dealing with customers, so providing systems that can improve any of these functions is critical to success.

CRM comprises of the business process, the technology, and the rules required to deal with a customer at various stages of the business lifecycle. These transcend departments and, to a certain extent, any individual department function. For the best results in Customer Relationship Management, systems contain most of the data associated with the customer, but only deliver the view most relevant for a particular function. For example, a salesperson using a CRM in the mid-West of the United States does not need access to all the information that is associated with the current sales situation of a client in London, England. However, they may need access to customer satisfaction data, or references to help close a deal. Being able to provide the relevant information at the right time is often the key differentiator of a successful system.

WHO IS THE KEEPER OF CRM?

One of the most complicated questions to answer in any CRM scenario is who owns the applications and drives the strategy. In the early 1990s, when many firms started to understand exactly how dissatisfied their clients were with company service and products, CRM was the solution that many turned towards. Usually, however, these solutions were "point solutions" addressing a particular problem and little else in the organization. Sales force automation and support center software were some of the first to tackle this issue, most of the systems being based on pre-Internet client/server architectures.

If CRM is to be implemented effectively across many business functions, then the ownership for these systems becomes distributed accordingly. Each of the business units needs to be involved depending on the breadth of the system. For example, sales and marketing should be tightly co-ordinated to ensure that marketing and sales management issues are knitted together in effective programs and program management. Many organizations will try and use a centralized approach to the IT support and management of the systems, thereby ensuring reliability and security issues for access to some of the operation's most confidential information.

TYPICAL APPLICATIONS

Some of the common applications that make up a CRM system today include the following.

» At the highest level a contact management system such as Outlook or ACT! can and has to be considered the basis of a CRM. Many smaller operations (and some bigger ones) have based most of their strategies on these desktop tools.
» Packaged applications that often need to be customized, such as software that links the sales force to a Website.
» Connectivity to Web-based contact centers, allowing staff and partners (where permitted) to view the relevant information from a client's database.
» Analytics software that identifies buying habits. This allows organizations to create considerable "cross-selling" operations and ensure that new products are presented to clients where appropriate.
» Self-service products that allow the client to do the searching and buying themselves. These fall into a variety of categories, from Web-based systems to self-service kiosks.

THE PAYOFF

In order to gain the real benefit of CRM, tremendous integration of various parts of the business is required. This enterprise approach has to be carefully considered. CRM can create huge payoff for clients, but the understanding has to be there to see how to broker a solution that is going to create value. Organizations such as BMC (an international software operation) have shortened sales cycles, increased productivity, and improved customer satisfaction because of an enterprise implementation of CRM solutions.

Like many enterprise applications, the greater the number of departments that are connected and databases consolidated, the better the Return on Investment. Yet despite these benefits, many companies are still holding off on selecting and implementing their CRM solutions. The significant change management programs that need to be agreed and delivered are one of the reasons for the hold back. Many organizations are reluctant to change the way they are doing business, and want to hold back because of the high failure rate associated with CRM. For this reason the marketplace growth rates appear to be very high, with many firms still "waiting in the wings" before they make their enterprise CRM moves.

THE CUSTOMER REVOLUTION

Patricia Seybold, a long time advocate of systems that support customers and of automating them, has been something of a leading light in defining what CRM is and why it makes sense. In her latest book, she lists three principles:

1 the customers are in control;
2 customer relationships count; and
3 customer experience matters.

All of these have a considerable impact on the issues of CRM, firms that have to position CRM decisions in the light of an overall customer management strategy. This strategy should be a direct outcome of building and developing CRM systems; they should support overall business goals. Seybold's premises also fall nicely into line with Gary Hamel's strategic thinking on business in general. He illustrates clearly that the association between the customer interface and the core strategy should be inexorably linked (see Fig. 2.1).

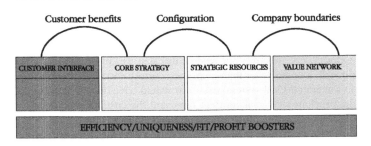

Fig. 2.1   Gary Hamel's view of creating competitive organizations.

Seybold believes and articulates strongly that the customers are in control. Citing the revolution sparked in the music industry that caused the industry to come to the customers, she notes that the power of the consumer and user is now unstoppable. The revolution that was caused by firms such as Napster providing individual downloads of tracks or songs created a demand that the music industry could not ignore. These customers have now driven a whole new set of demands that were not there before, including recordable CDs, download mobile players, and PDAs that support Web-based downloads.

The relationship between customer and suppliers should always have been high on the list of things for organizations to be concerned about; however, Seybold's take on this matter is clear. It costs money to acquire customers, and it costs even more to maintain these relationships. However, if the relationships are not maintained then the cost of reacquiring them, or replacing them with new ones is very expensive. This is called *customer capital*. Making customers valuable commodities might seem like an obvious deal for anyone, but even in the United States, where customer service is viewed as being at high standards, many firms fail.

Sometimes these failures result from not paying attention, and other times it is the lack of a co-ordinated CRM system. Recently my wife and I spent about five hours on the phone with various representatives of Chrysler Corporation dealing with the return of a Jeep at the end of its three-year lease. The lack of any type of integrated service management system, and different partners dealing with drop-off, inspection, and pick-up meant that each conversation with a new customer service representative meant starting over again. (Interestingly enough, the blizzard of sales information that battered the house prior to the lease end was very effective, but when a decision was made to replace the car with a brand other than Jeep, the courtesy ended.) If Chrysler had an integrated CRM system, each rep would have been able to notice the previous calls, making their reps' and the customers' lives easier. Business rules and processes can also cause major problems; in this example, there was no way to escalate a problem to a supervisor, thereby making it hard for the client to gain some level of improved service. Not to pick on Chrysler, but we were called again recently by another rep, trying to find out where the car had been inspected and dropped over a month ago. They had no record of where the vehicle was on the customer reps' system, yet made a final demand payment while the lease was still open and underway.

Understanding this total customer experience is much more than just making a good product, or providing the right information to those dealing with customers. However, the *customer experience* that Seybold highlights in her book has become more critical to the success of a company. Quality and service cause customers to change brand. A colleague who is a BMW fan told me he was bowled over by the attention he received at a Lexus dealership. Even though he was not really interested in the vehicle, the treatment and the entire customer experience made him consider a change.

The customer experience illustrates how important the process and customer treatment strategy is to the success of an organization. No amount of CRM technology alone will provide a substitution for great customer treatment. The processes and procedures have to be there, along with a culture of ''the customer does really matter.'' Seybold calls this a *branded experience*, and though the product may have a brand, the customer experience is almost as important as the product. Imagine a Rolls-Royce without superior service, or the Ritz with shoddy waiters – the experience and the product together create the brand.

Organizations have a tremendous opportunity to improve the way that they deal with their clients using CRM as a foundation, but it has to be built on solid footings: a customer-friendly culture and business procedures and processes to ensure that they come first.

The alignment of CRM technology, customer experiences, market needs, and a well-defined and differentiated product will build a brand, and a loyal one.

The Evolution of CRM

Customer Relationship Management has evolved over the course of the 1990s from specialized systems to the integrated systems of today. This chapter examines the evolution of the technology, its use and strategies for successful implementation today. It includes:

- » the history of CRM;
- » how the enterprise has used CRM;
- » the impact of the Web;
- » communication and collaboration tools;
- » authoring and content tools;
- » personalization and customization;
- » intranets and their impact on CRM systems;
- » finding and using the right information.

To help understand the current state of the art in CRM, it is useful to get some historical perspective on the topic. The market started in the late 1980s, primarily with players that developed "business function" software products. Their strategy was to penetrate and automate the CRM function of a particular department or business unit.

The primary goal of these software packages was to assist in the standardization and process automation of software systems such as customer support or sales force automation. Vendors such as Clarify, Siebel, and Vantive (now part of PeopleSoft) made up a good segment of this emerging market. Like vendors in other sectors of the market, the software was positioned as an automation tool.

Software that focused on the developing segments of customer support and sales force automation was deployed in Local Area Networks, based mainly on client/server solutions. Often the products required the company to change the way their operations functioned, by using workflow and procedural tools built into the products.

These early systems included functionality to allow clients to customize these business functions, within the context and capabilities of the systems. Typical features included:

» creation of sales scripts and customer support scripts for telephone sales and support;
» workflow software to determine the various stages of a sales or support process, sometimes with the relevant forwarding of information relevant for that process;
» business rules to ensure that the "system" did not become a barrier to the successful resolution of a customer problem, or lead management; and
» pipeline and sales management tools, built into the SFA (sales force automation).

User-based access to information was also a common feature of the more complex products.

In general, these systems were point solutions, and tended to be deployed in situations where there were already significant sales or support management problems that the software could potentially rationalize. At this early stage of the CRM market, from the late 1980s to the early 1990s, the segment started to gain traction but still had some significant limitations.

THE ENTERPRISE

The first major change in evaluation from the departmental systems, was the move to extending the capabilities of the systems to meet more than one business function need. This trend provided both benefits for the vendors (who could extend their reach and client base) and their customers, who could amortize the benefits of CRM to a larger group inside the company. During the mid-1990s many vendors tried to make this move, as more companies realized the benefits of keeping customer information in a centralized (or common) repository. This removed the potential for duplicate (and also inaccurate) information to reside in different systems according to business function: sales, marketing support, etc.

Another factor that encouraged the move to the enterprise at this time was enterprise ERP and data warehousing initiatives. These systems, now well established in the marketplace, were making the case that organizations could not change the way they were operating unless they had access to information about what was happening in the operation. While their vendors made progress connecting plan-ning, resources, and manufacturing functions across organizations, little was being done to connect the customer information associated with them.

Customer information was also very important to making these connections occur; after all, if you cannot connect inventory with sales demand, this can cause considerable problems. Likewise, the information that is captured at the support level frequently provides excellent input to manufacturing and engineering for changes to be made.

Industries with shorter, high demand lifecycles tended to be some of the early adopters of this enterprise class CRM software. Unfortu-nately, many of these early ''multi-function'' systems did not meet the requirements for all of the organization. As many had come from some business function preference (sales or support), the modules that they implemented tended to be less than perfect for the area that was not their core capability. While the applications often addressed a real business need, they also had the characteristic of being expensive to buy and maintain.

These early systems were always focused on business process improvement in individual segments, but did not deal with the enterprise issues very well.

It was around this same time that vendors were extending their offerings, and Internet-based systems first appeared. The Web-based entrants created a lot of opportunity but also tremendous confusion and frustration in the marketplace.

There were two major problems for the vendors in the marketplace at that time.

1 How to migrate an existing architecture to support Web-based functionality?
2 How to deal with the integration issues of these other products and services?

The first point would be a particular thorn in the side for many vendors. Web architecture was already gaining considerable momentum at this stage, particularly in the area of intranets. Often at a fraction of the cost of other client/server solutions, rudimentary intranets were popping up all over organizations, making it easy for content to be posted and distributed through the operation.

Operations were starting to understand that the benefits associated with Web-based solutions were considerable. The communications potential for attracting new clients, self-service applications, and the sheer size of the Web created a huge new level of activity in the marketplace.

THE WEB

As the Web entered the picture, it changed everything. Suddenly the rules for the use of the technology had changed radically. Up to this point CRM was an automation tool, a business improvement tool, but mainly for internal purposes. Suddenly we were faced with new applications that allowed the client to make the decision right there: to buy something on the Web, to gain access to the data to solve a problem, to communicate with others.

It had to change from that point on. CRM needed to be facing the customer as they were making the buying decision; being hidden in the back office would not cut the mustard. It had to migrate to the Web. Individuals needed their account information to be captured at the point of sale, and the communication and interaction explosion of the Web happened in early 1995.

COMMUNICATION AND INTERACTION TOOLS

Key to any successful customer relationship is the issue of communication tools. In addition to the standard fare of e-mail and browser-based solutions, vendors were now offering many different types and styles of communication and interaction tools that could assist in the development of partnerships.

These tools come in all shapes and sizes, including:

» project management
» project collaboration
» chat and instant messaging
» remote application access
» e-learning systems
» Webcast systems
» broadcast tools
» Web audio and radio
» Web video and Webcams
» customer support
» interactive sales support.

This abundance of tools assisted in the development and delivery of information for CRM activities. Figure 3.1 makes it clear that good use of these technologies can be made at all stages of the process. From development to implementation, collaboration tools can assist dramatically to reduce cost in all aspects of information delivery. In addition, they can be used to assist in the acceleration of sales cycles, and extensively through the support of new products as they are released to the marketplace.

Software and dedicated dotcoms made the greatest use of collaborative and remote access tools in the development of their customer

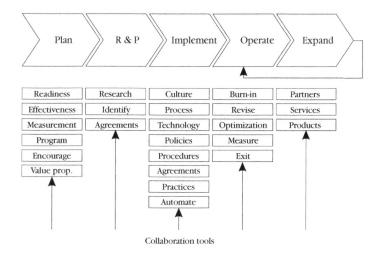

Fig. 3.1 Collaboration tools can assist at all stages of CRM development.

strategies. However, they are not alone in the creative use of tools that allow partners and clients to make decisions and provide solutions remotely.

New e-learning tools are also revolutionizing the way that business is operating. The high-tech industry has been a user of distance learning tools to improve the way that information about their products is distributed to the marketplace. Initially these tools were focused primarily on marketing-related information, with guided tours of products, places, or services delivered via the Web. The market is now moving to a new point, where support information, procedures, and certification is now possible with Web-based courseware and tools in the marketplace.

Customer support and helpdesks are also turning to these tools to assist with the support of their partner networks. Early studies show the use of collaborative tools, such as instant messaging or live chat sessions, demonstrates that many more customer calls can be handled by a service representative than via the phone (where calls are dealt with in a serial manner). The other advantage of this method of dealing with customer requests is that the entire chain of questioning and response are captured ready for analysis or re-use.

Similar options are being offered in self-service sales cycles, where prospective clients can gradually escalate the interaction with the Web environment, from e-mail to instant chat to speaking with a live sales representative. Sales studies show that up to 50% of sales staff activities are associated with supporting administration, not live face-to-face time with clients. The use of collaborative technologies could dramatically improve this ratio, with careful implementation in individual sales and partner cycles.

In partner situations, this is even more important, as there are usually fewer staff to support the partners inside the organization, making the efficiency factor more critical.

DEALING WITH DATA FOR PARTNERSHIPS

To a large degree, the selection of the system will depend on the sophistication of the partner information and how much access is required from the partners to internal systems. The CRM will need to support segmented access to data that partners need to update and change on a regular basis. Depending on the type of partnership, this may be sales, distribution, marketing, order entry, or inventory data. Obviously, this is technically more complicated than just access to the CRM and the fields therein.

In cases where the partner is going to provide end-user or other B2B information, then a more refined set of controls will also be needed from the system. Situations that require this level of information access will also require the work process to be carefully defined.

Partners will then be able to update this information remotely, thereby keeping the database up to date and in good working order.

AUTHORING TOOLS AND CONTENT MANAGEMENT

Authoring systems and content management were at one point mutually exclusive. The evolution of systems in this space has sustained a lightning pace. One reason is that many authoring systems are designed with the task of building the Website and not with maintenance, and/or creation of dynamic content. Many of these simple authoring systems run out of steam once more customization is needed or the volume of data increases.

Organizations should consider the development of systems with a clear view of content management and maintenance in mind. Otherwise, Websites that are developed fall into the category "static and difficult to update." We all know what happens to Websites that become stale. They do not create interest and lose traffic rapidly.

Each of the systems include the following elements:

» a Web server;
» application development tools;
» a database to drive the system; and
» authoring and maintenance tools.

Separation of the requirements for authoring the Website and its maintenance is the reason many organizations have been very frustrated with the performance of their initial efforts on the Web. The reason is that the development of the site concentrated on the issues of design and getting corporate brochureware on the site rather than providing good, relevant content for the users. Another reason is that authoring system vendors have tended to concentrate on the development of sites that best suit their tools and capabilities (no surprise here) and not on overall market requirements.

The Web server is the publishing center of any e-commerce system, and is the crucial delivery vehicle for information stored in the system. Driving this content to the Website and keeping it relevant for the application is the definitive goal for most organizations.

Content Management Systems have emerged as the standard method of dealing with the complex authoring, management, updating, and distribution problems associated with powerful Websites. Using these systems, organizations can keep catalogs, customer information, price lists, and other important B2B content up to date.

Customers using Content Management Systems want control and speed. They also want quality and customization of both content and appearance. Fortunately, with the modular nature of many Content Management Systems, it is possible to have it all.

Content Management Systems enable the business to:

» control the authoring and updating process;
» include data from many sources;
» manage the data presentation;
» enable distributed updating;
» post new changes quickly yet in a customized manner; and
» repurpose the data to differing sites and applications.

CONTENT MAINTENANCE AND DYNAMIC DELIVERY

The control of content maintenance and the dynamic delivery of information has made today's content management systems a must for most large scale web applications. Content maintenance and delivery has become the major issue for most business organizations.

Content maintenance provides the ability to update content remotely on a controlled basis, and has rapidly become the standard method of doing business. Some applications, such as auctions, only function if all participants can input and change data dynamically as a part of the process. Delivering the right content to the person who needs it at the time that they require the information is the aim.

Increasingly, market requirements are moving towards dynamic Web publishing. This permits operations to produce content "on the fly" from databases programmed based on the requirements of the user. This capability provides the foundation of all personalization and customization systems.

Systems that support dynamic Web publishing have some common attributes, including:

» a multi-media storage and management capability – this includes, text, graphics, video/audio, animation, and data related to page style and scripting for the application;
» using relational databases to manage the direction and layout changes for the content in the application;
» dynamically creating new pages based on user and predefined requests for content;

» creating new index or reference pages from stored content, including hyperlinks and cross-reference information; and

» automatically updating the Website based on remote authoring privileges.

Most systems now allow the creation and editing of Web environments with remote updating capabilities without the need for technical personnel. Workplaces require the facility to update the site information by the relevant staff inside the organization and not to create some huge technical bottleneck at the Webmaster's desk. The right content management systems will help businesses achieve this goal. These allow site updating tools to be driven deeply into the organization. Editorial and business controls are layered into these software systems, thereby providing critical controls for updates and security of the data in question.

The good news is much of this updating and changing can be done without the need for technical skills or any HTML or XML coding knowledge. After content changes are made, a new version of the site can be produced dynamically directly from the database without further ado, with all the style, content, indexes, and hyperlinks to associated content. Organizations today are looking for even more control, to ensure that the content is further refined to individual or workgroup needs. These features are known as personalization and customization.

PERSONALIZATION AND CUSTOMIZATION

Personalization and customization are features designed to improve the experience of the individual user of the site. In some cases this is managed by software "testing" the behavior of the user. This is done by capturing navigation patterns through the site, or buying preferences. Some sites will allow the user to self-select how they want to use the site, by identification of a particular "view" or path that has been prepared from them. Self-service applications with these features are becoming very popular throughout the e-business world.

Many software products will allow users to do even more than this, through the use of "profiling" software and agents resident on the Website. These agents will match your behavior, likes, and dislikes and prepare a report for the organization, giving them high level marketing information about how their site is being used and received, and at a more detailed level, the ability to profile what you would like to see the next time you visit.

These profiles have long been in use in the B2C market, and have created some controversy due to the privacy issues associated with them. In the B2B world, profiles are generally a good thing for both the company and the B2B user visiting the site. For example, if you are a service engineer continuously visiting a partner's site to find out information about products you are servicing, having the most relevant areas and news appear based on your needs will be a productive feature. It will also help ''push'' bulletins and changes directly to you, allowing preventative maintenance to occur where appropriate.

Many of these personalization profiling tools are designed to gather and store critical information without reducing a site's performance.

Powerful systems enhance this information by creating a visitor registry for incoming visitor data, a content catalog for the taxonomy of content on the Website for use in personalization, and a personalization/customization module to create the content to match the user profile.

Depending on the sophistication of the system involved in this process, a tremendous amount of customization can be achieved, in many cases much more than would be considered possible. Some of the options include:

» agents that will recommend content to visitors;
» management agents that will track where the visitor is in an electronic sales cycle (how many times they visited, what they were interested in, where they came from, where they went to);
» search tools that will provide results relevant for a particular community for affiliate group;
» tools to modify the content delivery according to new tastes, behavior, or instructions from the visitor;
» the ability to deliver content in different languages, based on the browser characteristics or visitor location; and
» the delivery of anticipated relevant content, for example, the five top FAQs could be delivered to a visitor to a B2B site.

There are limits to what can be done on the personalization and customization front, but we are nowhere near them at this point. Soon, all content and Web-based experiences will become customized, and the systems and the way they work will continue to expand and evolve.

DIFFERENT SYSTEMS FOR DIFFERENT TASKS

Each of the content management systems on the market has evolved from some point of reference in the way they developed. While Table 3.1 does not specifically include or exclude individual systems out there in the market, some are better suited than others for individual tasks.

Table 3.1 Examples of content management alternatives and where to use them.

Customer application	Application characteristics	Best suited system
Technical publishing, database publishing, knowledge management applications	High volume electronic document applications. Built-in sophisticated information retrieval and PDF generation	Document-oriented content management
Catalogs, B2B communication, supply chain, and distribution applications	Customization of content and presentation can be controlled interactively; business rules can be developed and modified easily; high level of personalization	Business-oriented content management
Commercial publishing, electronic magazines, and personalized content	Customized content can be presented in many different forms and formats	Publishing-oriented content management

The other important aspect of content management is where the data resides. If most of the data that you want to access is already housed in some internal system, this may be the source and platform that you want to use to drive your content management strategy and system.

INTRANET INFORMATION REPOSITORIES

Intranets can also fall into this category of a structured information repository. However, unlike the standard document management repositories, intranets come with other collaborative tools particularly attractive to partner relationships. Chat, bulletin boards, mail list servers, and newsgroups all provide an excellent method for the sharing and interaction of information between groups.

During the past several months, the Application Service Provider has also become a deliverer of intranets to the desktops of organizations around the United States. The concept of the remote intranet is still catching on, and the business models that support these systems are still emerging. Even ones with larger user bases, such as hotoffice.com, have found themselves as casualties of business models that cannot make money in time periods acceptable to their investors (despite a good product and 300,000 users). However, the concept of providing the relevant information for a partnership in a controlled extranet along with many other collaborative tools for the partnership still holds well.

As the intranet is already Web-based, there are considerable advantages to the development of solutions based on this platform. Here are a few of them:

» faster to deploy;
» easier to customize for different partner needs/presentation;
» scalability;
» easy to distribute software and data (Web-based);
» permits interaction with other systems;
» supports distance learning (distribute policies/procedures and information);
» some collaboration tools included.

Many systems will use a hybrid approach, where a portal solution includes elements from structured repositories, partner-specific extranets, and other sources in a browser system. The standard stuff that comes with most intranet solutions makes it a great solution for many organizations to start the development of their systems.

As Table 3.2 illustrates, there is a lot of value for money in a scalable package that can be integrated into a partner-specific solution relatively easily. The good news is there are many other alternatives also in the ASP category.

Table 3.2 Applications for collaborative tools, and how they are being used.

Industry	Tools	Application
Construction	Webcams, project management, e-learning, Web casts	Collaborative project management, site and construction reviews with partners, proposal development, etc.
Software	Demonstrations, trial downloads, sample, e-learning, etc	Sales and partner support
Financial	Product demonstrations, Web casts, newsletters, e-mail	Client and partner support for agents re-marketing their services

FINDING AND MINING THE INFORMATION

Organizing the information so that others can consume it easily makes perfect sense. Making this happen requires other tools to assist in the cataloging and retrieval of the relevant data. Information retrieval tools can also help with a knowledge management strategy by assisting users to find information that can subsequently be further catalogued or included in the KM repositories.

Every KM repository and relevant databases should be indexed using information retrieval technologies. The indexing engines (sometimes called spiders on the Web), will create indexes of the words and where they occur. This will then provide another method for partners and their clients to find relevant information that cannot be easily obtained through the organizational interface that you have provided with the system. And there will always be cases that this is so. Unless everything is catalogued in a common manner and a common framework (such as a library), it will be almost impossible to find every potential useful source of information without indexing the entire database.

As we know, once indexing engines start to work on very large datasets, they then start to provide increasingly less useful results. A simple search on the Web is a great example of this; a huge indexed source, producing huge results, most of which will be useless to the searcher, unless they use the more powerful filters and tools of the system.

When building large partner databases, it is very important that the indexing tools produce results that are relevant for the partners, and that this is done quickly. Partners, like most people using Web systems, have very little patience with Web-based systems. They want accurate results and they want them quickly. In addition, internal users of the KM system will also want to be able to identify potential candidates for searches and information results that can support their own activities internally in the business, and support their business partners.

The information retrieval technology can also operate in a proactive manner. Results of search activities can also produce pointers regarding areas of the knowledge management system that will need to be expanded. Finding out what clients are searching for and if those results have created success for them will show the way for changes in both content and navigation for many Web-based applications.

Data mining tools fall into another class of technology products. These are used to assist power users, and others looking for relevant information to create new segments of the knowledge base easily.

Once the domain of very large systems, with price tags to match, data mining solutions are becoming much more affordable in recent years. While the very sophisticated mining and analysis used in research applications and for the largest corporate databases are still in the category of six and seven figure investments, good desktop and LAN-based alternatives are now on the marketplace.

Data mining tools can also show where information relevant to a particular topic is located and do so very quickly. The relationships between the information sources can also be easily established and, with user interaction, individuals can find information that has not been well cataloged in their systems.

Combined, all of these systems now make up the elements that knit and feed around a modern CRM system and strategy. Some are very complex, others simpler, but they all have the same goal in mind. To serve the customer better.

The E-Dimension

CRM and the Internet create new opportunities for managing and dealing with existing and new customers. This chapter explores the key issues, including:

» why organizations need to use the Internet and CRM together;
» e-marketing and why it needs to be integrated with CRM;
» integration with other internal systems.

IMPLICATIONS OF THE INTERNET FOR THE SUBJECT AND ISSUES IT RAISES

As we discussed in Chapter 3, CRM technology combined with the Web, that has allowed us to communicate, influence, and transact on-line, has changed everything. Most business owners doing business with others already understand this reality: *there are huge efficiencies to be made by improving the way their businesses work with clients*. Ask anyone today and they will tell you that a great staff, a good plan, and excellent market conditions can make a successful firm. Absolutely next on this list are great customers and customer relationships. After many years of neglect, customers and their real value are given the visibility they deserve.

WHY ORGANIZATIONS NEED CRM

CRM systems become a key information food chain that feeds an organization's growth and market value. Each of these systems operates with a combination of business rules, technology infrastructure, and processes to deliver results to the organization. It is often difficult for organizations to view these systems in context, mainly because the rules of the market and the way that the technology is applied changes so rapidly.

Most organizations will develop a CRM strategy for one of two purposes:

1 to improve the operation of their internal business operations;
2 to operate in new segments of the marketplace with partners to reach more clients in the marketplace.

Market conditions often dictate that change has to occur and it has to happen quickly, particularly when we view the e-business issues of CRM. Factors include:

» a dramatically changing economy;
» much lower barriers of entry to enter a market;
» the ability to build for business in a specialized and fragmented market on a global basis;
» understanding of the value of managing the customer base effectively;

» technology confusion;
» the organization's ability to change the way they are doing things; and
» globalization.

Each of these factors has a moderate impact on the rate of change in a business sector; together they cause a veritable explosion of change. Organizations have traditionally ensured that their products and services were competitive in markets and environments that have been relatively stable. This is no longer the case. New technologies have allowed organizations to create partnership networks to leverage the power of suppliers and consumers, and more.

While few would disagree that the Internet is a global instrument of change, the crossing of international boundaries is just another example of how quickly and completely the competitive landscape can change for an organization. In B2B markets alone, one of the major sectors affected by partnerships and business relationships are expected to reach the $4trn mark within the next 24 months in the United States alone. Europe, somewhat the laggard in the development of this market, is now moving ahead at full steam. As markets and the leadership companies continue to grow, reasons appear for how they are taking the lead. CRM systems and the programs to support them will have made the difference for many of them.

While many firms want to see a clean transition to new business networks, the reality is that many of the matches are not there. There are new mechanisms that are simply not available in the old world model. Regardless of how much you may want to tell the existing bricks-and-mortar firm not to worry, the reality is that there is plenty to worry about.

The elements of the new business network have some specific characteristics. Successful entrants in this space will typically:

» employ leading edge technologies;
» outsource many aspects of their solution;
» worry about being a "first mover" in their market space;
» try and do something radically different to support new and different business processes in the target market; and

» know the value of customers and business partners and build programs to support them "first" in their rollout of the system.

Firms that have first mover status typically win, and the others come a very poor second place. While this rule is not yet proven in the incumbent space of the "establishment end" of e-commerce, supply chain B2B, it has proved so in other markets.

The B2C market has established winners, with little hope for those behind them. For example, Amazon was the winner in the book business, AOL won the on-line war, (does anyone remember Prodigy?), eBay won the auction battle. B2B exchanges are currently engaged in a similar turf conflict, with some early winners starting to emerge. Note how many of these early winners have come from a previous bricks-and-mortar background. Not many, but that does not mean that some will prevail.

If the business network is the framework of the future, then customers, and the way they interact with the organization, must be considered the lifeblood of the entire process. Customers, and the supporting business processes, provide the oxygen to the body, they keep a business vibrant and lively; they provide revenue and the reason that the firm is operating.

CUSTOMER RELATIONSHIP MANAGEMENT IS AN ENTERPRISE ACTIVITY

Customer relations are not a single dimensional issue. In an almost classic comparison to the issue of partner management, customers can affect and influence many parts of an organization. Most of what has been written on the subject of CRM has a single dimension. CRM for sales. CRM for marketing. CRM for support. Sound familiar? Until recently we viewed customer management as a sales issue. Not any more. We now understand we have many dimensions to our customer relationships. Sales, marketing, support, finance, contracts, et al. We are beginning to understand the value of that multi-dimensional relationship with our clients. Why? Because it costs us lots of money to acquire them, and even more when we lose them. Keeping them happy means doing so after the first sale, which will lead to the second, and the next, and so on. Not very complicated, but it has taken a long time for the technology, work process, and business practices to move into place to support these themes. Three years after its first release Patricia Seybold's *Customers.com*[1] is still a best selling book.

Similarly, partners have a common theme. They can be in many parts of the business, have a small or large impact on the sales, marketing, selling, or distribution of a product. These partners affect a business in different ways according to their role in the business network. The members of this network now include the following:

» the manufacturer;
» the developer;
» the distributor;
» the intermediary;
» the customer;
» the outsourcer;
» supply chains;
» distribution chains;
» the affiliate; and
» the consultant.

These various members become somewhat organized through the development of the business network set up by the company. Dependent on their role, these partnerships control the way that the client operates in the market. In fact, the interdependency of a business on others becomes a major factor in its ability to service the market effectively. Those that cannot make it happen may suffer the consequences. The result is the evolution of dedicated *business networks* for the organization, using e-commerce technology as the foundation for their development and evolution. This modern business network is a combination of suppliers, buyers, customers, facilitators, trading centers, stores and more.

E-MARKETING

Today's CRM vendors, and others in the e-marketing space, are trying to provide a seamless set of services to allow organizations to quickly take advantage of the information contained in the CRM itself. Based on the interaction with the CRM system, software can interpret what to do next to assist in the leverage of the relationship. In the case of e-marketing systems, this could be the automated response for an existing client expressing interest in a new product, or an upgrade to an existing one. The profile of the client's activities can create the necessary flags to trigger actions in systems outside the CRM, but is dependent on it to supply the right data. For example, a vendor sells a specific class of product, the company is bringing a new version to the market, and wants to let this partner know about what is coming soon. Perhaps this will be included in a special offer allowing the partner to "trade-in" an existing product, or upgrade with a discounted coupon. By performing a search of relevant targets in the CRM, the information to create a specialized e-mail campaign can be easily created. Then, by taking the information from the CRM, the partners can then target their own clients easily. This profiling of accounts inside the CRM and providing feedback from the results of an e-marketing campaign can create tremendous value for all concerned.

If "permission marketing" is enacted, then the issue of "spam" or other irritating unsolicited materials is not in question, thereby serving the end client, the partner, and the originator of the material. Increasingly, these e-marketing systems are either becoming modules of the larger scale systems, or they are easy add-ons to existing information sources. Application Service Providers are providing new tools to dramatically reduce the entry costs of such systems. Typical add-on e-marketing tools include:

» e-mail marketing and management systems;
» Website tracking and statistical analysis tools;
» newsletter creating and marketing tools;
» coupons;
» advertising management tools;
» content re-licensing tools.

One of the most powerful mechanisms in this marketplace is the use of one-to-one marketing systems. The concept of one-to-one marketing is now well developed in the current marketplace, and most CRMs will provide the mechanism to leverage it.

One-to-one also makes tremendous sense as the basis for partnership strategies, since the tools that allow for the customization of information to various sources are the very same ones used to develop individual marketing and product messages and offerings via the Web. The masters of one-to-one are found in both the B2C arena and the B2B marketplace. Amazon, a well-documented case to be sure, has created the benchmark by which many other systems are measured. They profile clients and visitors, then continue to refine the presentation of products, information, and special offers according to the customer's preferences. Beyond this, they have created communities of like buyers, so individuals can see what others in similar demographics or interest areas are purchasing. This is a complete cycle: individual requirements are personalized; individuals are grouped into communities; finally, their membership is re-marketed to them. You have to admire this seamless use of technology, demographics, and world-class marketing. Marketing and re-marketing at its best (Figure 4.1).

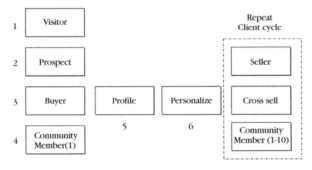

Fig. 4.1 Amazon e-marketing, turning visitors into customers into communities.

In addition to this superlative end-user marketing, Amazon understands partnerships and how they can leverage their business. Rather than trying to get everyone in the world to visit their site, Amazon instead focuses on allowing others to participate in the transaction.

Their affiliate program has more than 50,000 members. By giving up to 15% of the transaction to firms that refer customers, they create another element of loyalty and also allow others to advertise relevant Amazon products via their Websites. Other B2B firms such as Cisco have also performed great feats of e-marketing using one-to-one technologies and systems for their business partners. Another firm with a large amount of partners, Cisco has the added problem of a very complex product offering, requiring much assistance with configuration and control to ensure that the right items are being ordered and will work together. By using a combination of one-to-one, CRM, and externalizing an internal configuration management system, Cisco partners have a very powerful and jaundiced view of the world. Powerful, because they know that when they are ordering their Cisco system configuration that it will be available, that it will work, and what impact this has on their partner relationship (discounts etc); jaundiced, because other partners that they deal with for networking products have to climb a considerable wall to meet the level of self-service that Cisco is providing today. Loyalty and performance are being rewarded all around for Cisco as a result.

One confusing element in the decision-making process of CRM and e-marketing systems is the difference between customization and personalization. While it may appear obvious, the ability to handle both levels is very important for partnership relationships. If the system only supports customization at the company or department level, there will be no opportunity to further filter how a specific message can be delivered to an individual in an organization, thereby limiting the ability to service either the partner or their clients more effectively. Even if an organization only requires the former at the beginning of the system implementation, then consideration should be made for system expansion later in the process.

Metadata (data about the data) is another immensely useful by-product of these systems. With a good Web-tracking tool, providing feedback based on what worked and what did not can create tremendous input to marketing and support departments across the world. This information is also not just limited to Websites, where the traffic patterns and visitor flow are analyzed in detail. These tools can also track what is happening in e-mail campaigns: how many deleted the message before reading it, which links they liked and which ones were not visited, effectively how relevant the information was to the visitor. Used effectively, this information can create enormous benefit to the partner-driven organization. For organizations that are focused on self-service applications, this is particularly important, as they only really provide considerable benefits if users really "serve themselves." By tracking this behavior, operations can then improve each subsequent offering, or changes in the Website, allowing for lower marketing and/or support costs, regardless of the objective of the tool.

The net result of all this is that keeping e-marketing and CRM systems working together is very important if there is going to be an effective leverage of the technology and the systems, regardless of the tools that are used. As a result they can determine, through the combined use of e-marketing and CRM systems, how a prospect is using their system, and ultimately allow them to offer one-to-one offerings for the operation.

The ability to be able to customize the experience for the user is a critical element for success in the implementation of these systems. As most businesses have a wide range of contacts within their scope, effectively leveraging and managing this pool is of great importance to their ability to partner effectively. Just take the numbers of contacts that even the smallest organization comes into contact with over the course of a year. Aside from existing customers, there are prospects, leads from trade shows, professional contacts, and personal contacts. How many of these are pooled into a central base where they can be leveraged for further use? E-marketing campaigns and other traditional means are often co-ordinated in a manner that will not leverage these relationships over the long haul.

At the most basic level the CRM is the repository of information to start this process; after all, we cannot market or manage the information if we have no way of even seeing what is happening at the contact level. Most organizations now understand the value of this data, and that it needs to be the starting point of any successful partner or client relationship system.

INTEGRATION WITH OTHER SYSTEMS (INTERNAL, XML AND PEER-TO-PEER)

While e-marketing systems are obviously a good starting place for integrating information, it is not the only one. As earlier diagrams and narrative indicate, linking CRM data with relevant information from other internal and external systems is important to the real success of the application.

For the internal data, this could be coming together in a seamless application such as a supply chain management system, providing the relevant access as determined by the CRM. It may also include access to information on an application-by-application basis, for example a partner's sales person checking on the inventory or availability of a product or service. Regardless of the requirement, the relevant data needs to be paired with the person that needs it rapidly.

External data, from others' systems, may be just as important to your partners as information that you are providing directly. This might be safety information, product descriptions (in the case of a reseller), legal documents, or logistics support for delivery and storage. As we look at completing the food chain of information to many clients then the external data has to be included. One acronym is being used more to effect this exchange of mission critical data, XML. Extensible Mark-Up Language has rapidly become the standard and instrument of change for meeting these mission critical business needs. While EDI (Electronic Data Interchange) ruled the private networks for many years, XML has rapidly established itself as the standard to allow business networks between firms and industries to talk the same language, and thereby integrate this all-important data.

Another factor for the integration has been the recent rise in the development of peer-to-peer networks. The real reason for the creation of peer-to-peer over the Internet may never be known, but there is no question that they work. One of the most famous implementers of peer-to-peer networks is Napster.com; the now famous story of the 19-year-old founder, creating a network of 35 million users, without a file to be seen on their computers. Their peer-to-peer network works based on Napster hosting the directory and the files (in this case MP3 music files) situated on millions of computers spread around the Internet. Sounds wild, but it works. When Napster was in its heyday it often had peak loads of one million downloads per hour. This could not be done any other way without spending huge sums of money on computers, storage, management, and bandwidth. The peer-to-peer model does not require much of any of these elements, as users make a direct connection with the other system through a hyperlink or program, and then the peer-to-peer thing starts to happen. The computer making the connection starts the application with the connection on its peer (hosting the data or application). That's it. So simple you may wonder why it has not been done before. Well, as with many good ideas it has been. Peer-to-peer networks were commonplace in the early local networks, with one PC talking to another, sharing bandwidth on the network, sharing files and sometimes applications. The difference this time of course is the size of the network, the Internet. Very large, and very scalable.

Whether information is shared internally, externally using XML or a state of the art P2P system, the need to identify the relevant information to be shared and the means to integrate it is a key starting point. Ultimately, using the CRM as a focal point for the individuals, their roles, and the organizations and what they should have will create benefits for all in the long term.

NOTE

1 Seybold, P.B. (1998) *Customers.Com*. Random House, New York.

The Global Dimension

Customer Relationship Management offers great opportunities to go global. These include:

- » why the world is spending big money on CRM;
- » global integrated strategies;
- » partner management and internal efficiency;
- » internationalization, keeping systems talking the right language;
- » international distribution models and their impact on CRM;
- » product suitability;
- » pricing and legal factors;
- » cultural and work process concerns.

CRM has been growing in both understanding and importance as organizations apply it to their operations. The global reach of the Internet and in particular communication technology allows others to comparison search and make decisions about how they will buy and distribute products.

By now, most companies have implemented some form of CRM activity. For many, an important aspect of this decision was the capability to go worldwide with an effective strategy to manage their clients and their relationships. In order to achieve accelerated sales cycles, potential clients have to see more information in order to make decisions quickly. Meanwhile, corporate concerns about comparative shopping and the public broadcast of previously "private" information all gnaw at the current culture of the organization.

THE WORLD IS SPENDING BIG MONEY ON CRM

CRM as an industry itself is huge: recent estimates show the European market alone should hit the $34bn level by 2001, according to a studies by IDC (International Data Corporation). In the European market, there has been considerable failure as well as success with CRM, and inadequate training has taken a large part of the blame for the failures. As with many failed US systems, organizations are focused on CRM as a way of methodically institutionalizing good practices and process to help with the leverage of client relationships. In fact, worldwide, organizations are beginning to understand that much of the value of CRM comes from leveraging relationships and creating customer satisfaction, rather than just automating and improving internal functions.

INTEGRATED STRATEGIES

Many global organizations continue to struggle with the number of options that are available to them. As CRM has moved from an inward-facing technology, many operations now understand that only integrated strategies will produce the results that they need from CRM. Traditional contacts with clients – face-to-face meetings, the phone, and the fax machine – are being complemented by the Internet, wireless, and broadcast medias that have become very affordable. Many operations are considering these collaborative technologies as important as the actual transaction technology that lets the client order the product directly from the Web.

As more companies look to CRM as a method of being able to service their clients more efficiently, the payback at the international level becomes considerable.

IT'S NOT ALL ABOUT AUTOMATION

International operations in particular have understood the value of the personal touch, so creating a balance between the technology and the human aspect of CRM is key to success. Merely automating the function, and trying to keep the customer away from high touch points in the organization does not achieve the goals. This lesson has been learned in Europe, and now Asian operations are starting to view CRM as a key strategy to drive growth, increase loyalty, and improve customer satisfaction. As the economy around the world makes it easier for others to find and change suppliers, and an expanding consumer base becomes available outside traditional markets, CRM has a big role to play.

One trend in Asia identified by the Asia Pacific Research Group, is that of integration of the call centers with Websites. This trend follows the self-service trend of the US market in recent months, and ensures that the relevant information and the client profile are both serviced effectively.

Asian firms' goals from CRM include a highly integrated strategy to achieve success:

» integration of different data sources;
» integration with existing back office applications; and
» effective integration of different organizations and business functions within the corporation.

To support many of these issues in the global marketplace, India and the Philippines have been positioning themselves as leading locations for international call centers, making CRM a prerequisite for those operations.

The call center hardware and software market in Asia Pacific is expected to reach $656mn in 2005 (Asia Pacific Research Group).

However, if both countries are successful in their bids to be worldwide call centers for many US and European operations, then these numbers could be conservative.

PARTNER MANAGEMENT AND INTERNAL EFFICIENCY

The collaborative benefits of CRM for both external and internal use continue to drive spending and business improvements in CRM worldwide. In particular, firms are making use of CRM not only to improve the way their staff operate to support their clients, but also as the platform for supporting companies outside their operation.

Some companies want to make a rapid move to such an integrated approach, and organizations that are now providing CRM as an Application Service Provider can deliver results in very short timeframes.

Teraport, based in Germany, are a good example of a firm that has moved to a Web-based solution, with the hosting of their application outsourced to Salesforce.com. While many have become suspicious of the ASP business model, Salesforce.com has signed up some very large firms to their service, Time Warner, Siemens, and Autodesk to name a few. For the smaller or rapidly growing firm there is considerable advantage to using services such as these. Teraport, with a sales force spread around Europe and clients in the US, were looking for a system that would provide the virtual communications needed to grow their business.

More firms that have international needs may end up going along the ASP route. It certainly reduces some of the technology risk when building the system, and allows firms to gain the benefit of adding business functions (customer support, marketing) when they are ready to implement them. While many are skeptical about outsourcing their customer data, more firms are considering the ASP model.

INTERNATIONALIZATION

Many organizations have to make compromises when they create an environment that is going to go global. Ensuring that customer information can be accessed from many locations has complications. These have to be considered to ensure that the systems will be usable by all parties; otherwise, a huge amount of time and money can be wasted in the effort.

While many of these are important factors for any international enterprise deployment, they have particular concern for CRM-based applications. Many of the systems that work across many languages and cultures have to be conditions for compromise. Some firms will take the "Internet approach" and have the entire systems available in English language only. While this may work for some firms, it is not acceptable for many others.

Determining the timing and methods to implement CRM that will be successful can be a daunting task. The Web can be a short cut, but there is a huge difference between having an "informational site" and using the Web as an integrated part of a company's international business. CRM is a foundation in this process.

INTERNATIONAL DISTRIBUTION MODELS AND THEIR IMPACT ON CRM

An international e-business strategy changes how an operation is doing business in dramatic ways. Understanding what the requirements for such a change are needs careful consideration, and having the right CRM tools to help manage these changes are key.

As Table 5.1 indicates, some major changes have to be considered in the development of this strategy. For companies that already have international distribution in place, channel conflict can be a major concern. For new distribution strategies the other concern – of product support – will also play a major part in the development of the strategy.

E-BUSINESS GLOBALIZATION FACTORS

1 Distribution model
2 Product suitability
3 Legal and pricing
4 Localization
5 Transaction
6 Fulfillment

Table 5.1 Business model impact with international e-business. (Source: Harvard Computing Group 2001.)

Business model	Impact on direct sales to new international clients	Impact on current international channels	Impact on direct sales to current international clients
New international e-business business model	No channel conflict, but complete system from demand through fulfillment has to be developed	Not applicable	Not applicable
Existing direct business model (non Web-based)	Could create conflict with current distribution systems in place, if not factored into the design.	Not applicable	Could create conflict with current distribution systems in place, if not factored into the design.
Existing indirect business model	Could create conflict with current distribution systems in place, if not factored into the design.	Needs to be developed considering existing channels and support that are in place.	Could create conflict with current distribution systems in place, if not factored into the design.

PRODUCT SUITABILITY

Ensuring that a product is suitable for the target marketplace is the next step in the process. This includes a consideration of a number of factors, including some that are specific for e-business.

» *Pricing*: Is product competitive in local marketplace?
» *Competitiveness*: How should product be priced and packaged for local market needs?
» *Language*: Is localization required to enter the market? What is the cost and scope of translation needed for success?
» *Market size*: Is the marketplace large enough to warrant the investment?
» *Internet infrastructure*: Are there a suitable number of Internet users to make the transactions happen (including good connections via ISPs)?
» *Cultural infrastructure*: Is e-business accepted as a means of doing business? What is the current rate of e-business growth in this market?
» *Existing distribution systems*: Are there current distribution systems in place that will help (or hinder) an e-business initiative?
» *Shipping/fulfillment*: How will the product be shipped and delivered to the client?
» *Support*: What local support is required?
» *Volatility*: Is the market volatile? (Either financially or politically.)[1]

A CRM system will have an impact on how many of these issues are dealt with directly with the customer or the business partner. The size of the market, marketing initiatives, support programs, legal agreements, privacy issues, and even shipment have a huge impact on how a system should be built and developed.

Even the most heterogeneous of Web-based businesses, like Amazon or Yahoo! have localized versions of their products and supporting CRM systems. Research needs to be done to ensure that the organization will be successful in the development and delivery of the system. International CRM often becomes a national issue, with "my way is better than yours." With operations concerned about the business practices and security issues of CRM in various markets, care needs to be taken to ensure that acceptable marketing and sales practices are modeled into the solutions.

Most CRM products have considerable workflow and work process scripting tools available to allow different methods of information transfer to meet these needs. However, care needs to be taken to ensure that they meet legal requirements in the international market in play.

PRICING AND LEGAL FACTORS

Developing pricing strategies and packaging them into a CRM for international distribution via the Web is no more complex (or simple) than any other environment. However, if this is the first foray into the international marketplace, then several issues need to be determined.

The first phase will comprise of the basic business issues of: single or custom pricing strategy for each market; margin goals; cost of sale; cost of support; market share goals; transfer costs (if applicable); and wholesale and retail prices. Once these have been determined, other pricing factors come into play including: competition; what the current marketplace will stand; currency transactions; import duties; export duties; and shipping costs.

Many companies are concerned that once their US list price is shown on their site, then it will be very difficult to obtain a different (read higher) price from other markets. There is no question that once a US list price is shown, then a benchmark has been placed for international prospects to consider. However, there are other variables to consider that cause changes in price and support, for instance:

» *warranty*: increased price for international support;
» *one single price based on US list*: if the transaction is in dollars, no currency issues arise;
» *support*: local support has different price;
» *shipping and handling*: cost will increase based on client requirements (air or sea freight); and
» *customs and import/export duties*: usually paid by the consumer.[2]

Careful consideration of contract issues should be made to avoid potential problems. A good approach is to keep things simple and understandable. This will reduce confusion and potential problems.

Many countries have very different commercial trading practices, and it is important to become familiar with them before presenting them with an unsatisfactory method of purchase. The legal profession and governments worldwide are also trying their best to come to terms with the complex array of problems associated with trading on the Web – it changes many rules of trading that were based on the physical transfer of goods across borders for many years.

CULTURAL AND WORK PROCESS CONCERNS

In all things international, the cultural application of what should and should not be done remains critical to success. Because it is easy to offend others' expectations and requirements through misunderstanding, it is important to understand the basis of the business deal. Too many people fail to make the effort to understand international business concerns or are unwilling to adapt themselves to the realities of understanding cultures, customs, and languages in order to gain an advantage when doing business in different countries. When implementing CRM this is particularly important. For example, what the United States considers reasonable in terms of gaining access to personal information may be totally unacceptable elsewhere. Even the method of contact can have a considerable impact on how sales processes are supported.

Successful organizations make the effort to understand how they are going to work together and the needs of their international customers before they make their move. The businesses that do show interest in the people with whom they are dealing, know that it leads to additional business. Just as an individual has to adapt to the relevant protocols of each nation to become an effective communicator and businessperson, so companies using CRM have to do the same.

Most CRM systems involve considerable automation of existing manual or physical processes (sales and service for example), so making sure that these are acceptable to the target users and communities is essential. For example, the US consumer is much more likely to accept unsolicited mail, e-mail and telephone canvassing for products. In Europe this practice is frowned upon, and the government provide means for the individual to ''opt out'' of all systems.

In order to avoid some of these cultural issues the following best practices can assist considerably in the acceptance of products and services.

1 Understand local business practices and how they can be encapsulated in e-business systems.
2 Ensure that the quality of language translation and terms and conditions meet local requirements and relevant laws.
3 Product packaging and naming should be sensitive to regional concerns and practices.

NOTES

1 Source: Harvard Computing Group 2001.
2 Source: Harvard Computing Group 2001.

The State of the Art

Customer Relationship Management is constantly evolving. So what are today's hot topics in CRM? This chapter explores current trends, including:

» self-service CRM and how it works;
» CRM systems;
» sales and marketing;
» distribution support and supply chain;
» business intelligence;
» analytics and where to use them.

There are many issues facing us today in the application of CRM strategies and technologies. Viewing CRM as a way to improve the business's operation, two major trends emerge. These trends have a strategic as well as technological implication and they are: self-service, and integrating business intelligence tightly with CRM.

SELF-SERVICE

The Internet, and in particular, B2B and B2C e-commerce has produced some significant challenges for the development of rapid CRM programs. The real potential of self-service has been exploited in Web-based applications, such as those used by business exchanges, infomediaries, and Application Service Providers. Establishing relationships and determining sources of information or new products, tasks that used to take months of research and visits can now be conducted in hours and days via the Web. However, to make these relationships work and effectively simulate the appropriate business processes is not a trivial issue. However, it is the one that is addressed by self-service applications.

Organizations have built Web environments that target potential customers, move them through the education and benefits of doing business on-line and ultimately facilitate the agreement or transaction electronically. Behind every one of these self-service applications lies an integrated CRM solution.

What exactly do we mean by self-service? The Internet provides us with enormous value when we build the environment to support new ways of doing business. Of all of these, self-service is the most attractive business model. The telephone, the gramophone, and the television are all examples of self-service tools that improved communications and the range of our experiences. Because the Internet is multi-media, we have the opportunity to change the way that these interactions and experiences occur. By building systems that allow us to identify the transaction, the data, the people, the service, the results, it is easy to see how self-determination is possible with the computer. The connection between research, decisions, transactions, and recording is all in one location. We can service ourselves, gaining advice and recommendations based on how to make the decision, then execute the decision.

To fully understand the importance of self-service, we first have to re-establish some principles that have not been in vogue recently. Due to the meltdown of many dot-com enterprises in 2000–2001, some bricks-and-mortar firms are feeling comfortable with their position as people-intensive systems, not computer-based self-service. Some consider that this model will continue, to the point that dot-com self-service has had its day. Forget this advice. It is going to become very large, and new and renewed companies will embrace it in a big way.

SELF-SERVICE DIMENSIONS

Self-service applications allow organizations to achieve the following goals:

» improve the quality of service for applications that are repeatable and have defined procedures; and
» allow the volume of service to scale without adding large numbers of incremental staff

This alone should place CRM-based self-service high on the list for development in any organization. Often, self-service applications are relegated to those that cannot be developed with traditional systems. Companies like Cisco and many dot-coms have reversed this trend, realizing that there is no way for them to scale or provide the service to their partners and clients without self-service at the core of the strategy.

Self-service applications should be the ones that are sought out early in any CRM strategy. They will create value, codify knowledge, and improve customer service in a single stroke.

One major stumbling point for an organization in the development of these systems, is the reference points in the market. The fact that Cisco has succeeded may not instill confidence in the furniture maker in Ohio or the manufacturing company in Northern England. Since self-service systems require a complex blend of business, work process, and technology understanding, they have to emerge from the initiating firm with confidence. Part of this confidence can be built from a solid understanding of how the technology components work and interact. There is also a requirement to fully understand how work processes can be applied to the technology components in order to create the "electronic process" in a useful manner. That's the bad news; the good news is there are a lot of reference points out there today to look towards for guidance.

All or nothing?

Before moving too far along the self-service road, we also need to consider that self-service is both strategy and tool, and not an end unto itself. There is no reason why only a portion of a complete process or cycle should be made self-service or complemented with other systems.

Customer service applications are good examples of this category: information is made available to the customer network and then an escalation procedure allows them to back out to get real "help" on the telephone or via on-site visits. For the early-stage, diagnostic aspect of self-service (troubleshooting and problem solving) the customer can enter this information directly via the support system.

Each part of the process can be defined according to what makes sense for self-service applications. Some simple self-service applications are in the category of a "must-do". Downloads of corporate documents relevant for upgrading equipment in the field, material and safety data sheets, catalogs, etc., will usually not a take great deal of justification or analysis before deciding to make them self-service to your customers.

However, there are other cases where self-service will not be appropriate. As these occur, use other means and blend them into the process. In most situations, companies are looking for high quality responses in reasonable timeframes. By using self-service to automate many of these processes, improvements in timeframes and quality can be made simultaneously.

CRM

Of all of the applications that have a huge impact on partnership relationships, CRM to support customers and partners has the greatest potential for tremendous return on investment. Because of the high cost overhead associated with customer support applications, it can be relatively easy for organizations to create ROI in excess of 500%, or more.

Taking applications such as helpdesks, traditionally manned by telephone support, and moving many aspects of the service to the Web can change the entire customer support model for the better (see Table 6.1). Typical applications that meet these requirements would include ones that have a high amount of procedural requirements, and of course some level of repeatability for the target applications.

Table 6.1 Example of self-service application improvements over traditional telephony-based systems.

Existing environment	Self-service system	Benefits
Telephone help desk	On-line self-service knowledge base	Faster response to partners
	Frequency Asked Questions (FAQ)	Consistent response to questions and answers
	Searchable knowledge base	Policies and procedures are codified rapidly within in the environment
	Intelligent trouble-shooting system for resolving problems	Lower cost of response
	On-line chat and instant messaging to allow for interaction with partners as they need on-line assistance with other systems	Customer service reps can handle more calls
		Ability to add more data to internal and partner systems
		Ability to measure the responsiveness of the system

Customer support has a potential overabundance of self-service applications. Increasingly these are also being made available in the ASP model, where firms will offer products that allow an organization to use their Web response platforms as a baseline for self-service systems. This model, with many collaborative tools already included in the platforms, is becoming very popular for the development of partnership e-business systems. High value applications that should be considered include:

» e-learning for distance learning;
» e-mail responses and bulletins;
» newsletter and e-service bulletins driven by sign-up mail list servers;
» knowledge centers;
» Web broadcast technology;
» on-line help built into applications;
» on-line policies and procedures.

Most organizations have been focused on the low-hanging fruit of this application segment. However, planning in advance can save considerable dollars in the long run, and will also focus staff on dealing with the more severe problems as they arise. Most support staff do not enjoy having to answer the same question for the tenth time in a week. Capturing and re-using this information is key to the success of these systems, for both staff and the organizations interacting with them.

SALES AND MARKETING

For the dot-com companies that started out with a Web-based sales solution, they have never had to deal with the issue of whether the sales process should be dealt with by people or whether they should be self-service. The reason for this is most dot-coms have had no sales process to protect, and many of them rely much more heavily on "electronic visibility" on the Web to gain partners and clients.

New media magazines and individual industry periodicals have been the target of their advertising dollars, but much of the plan has been based on building partnerships via the Web. Affinity programs have become a mainstream way of gaining ground in the marketplace. Even a new start-up can get much of what they need to support parts of their e-marketing and sales strategies by using ASP services such as bcentral.com from Microsoft. Organizations offering self-service applications to set up search positioning, create ad campaigns, and manage e-mail marketing and customer support all have to utilize well integrated self-service. The prices of these ASP services are low to try and attract large numbers of users, therefore they *have* to be self-service to make the cost structure viable.

For the majority of firms that are looking at self-service sales, a hybrid model will be in place. While Amazon does have customer account reps, their sales model is to keep these down to a minimum.

Segmenting the sales activities so that elements of the process can be identified for their suitability to a self-service model is a useful exercise. In addition, when considering these elements, care should be considered if these elements will transfer to the potential partners end customer sales process. While this is an oft-neglected area, providing pre-designed sales process and e-business models for new business partners creates tremendous value.

By reviewing existing sales cycles and process (see Fig. 6.1), and identifying where the bottlenecks are in the process, candidates will surface for self-service sales applications.

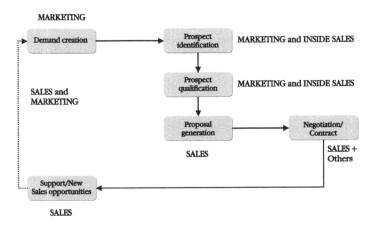

Fig. 6.1 Typical sales and marketing cycles.

Most sales activities are tightly integrated with marketing activities in the electronic cycle. As e-business tools are used to assist with the development and identification of new prospects in the business cycle they need to be tightly integrated into sales processes. This will ensure that they are not wasted.

Most self-service sales and marketing cycles focus on:

» shorter sales cycle;
» lower cost of sales;
» higher customer retention;
» cross-selling opportunities;
» faster qualification cycles; and
» self-service sales.

For partnership sales, the issue of who takes the order has always been a bone of contention. Depending on how the partnership has been organized, expectations of how sales will be handled, and by which party, will vary. In the case of business exchanges, where leads, buyers, and sellers intersect, the lead-giving organization will often take the front position. In other circumstances, such as a supply chain, leads may come from the partner to the supplier. In each situation the optimized strategy will be dependent on these relationships (see Table 6.2). For many situations, the following will represent excellent opportunities for either complete or partial self-service solutions in the sales and marketing areas:

Table 6.2 Self-qualification and electronic sales process.

Existing environment	Self-service system	Benefits
Self-qualification	Self-registration for company information	Driven to Website via other source
	Sign up for product demonstrations and or sales follow-up	Customer brings themselves through the demonstration cycle
	Self-demonstration or viewing of product using Web-assisted technologies	Faster sales cycle
	Comparison shopping guide	Objections are dealt with on-line
	Request for quote	Potential for self-configuration (e.g. Dell, Lands' End)
	Self configuration	Close the deal electronically
	Place order	

By providing this information on-line it is possible to go well beyond the self-qualification stage, right though to purchasing and fulfillment of the order. Other opportunities in the self-service category would include:

» e-marketing
» Web seminars
» sales presentations
» business exchanges
» pricing
» configuration management
» inventory information
» scheduling
» shipment data
» business intelligence applications
» market research.

The more sophisticated applications obviously require tight integration with some of the back office systems. Data for inventory, product shipment scheduling, and requirements for special orders, all need to be tightly integrated with the systems that hold this data. Firms such as Dell Corporation have brought this type of self-service selling to a new level in their direct client base, but have also optimized the back office systems into their suppliers' systems to make the entire thing work.

INTEGRATION OF CRM

Distribution support and supply chain applications

A major part of any customer success, particularly distribution-oriented systems, require access to much internal information for the system to work, such as catalogs, price lists, configuration management systems, and all sorts of training and information transfer programs to support these efforts.

Fortunately, with the use of sophisticated content management tools available in the market today, the same information can be re-used time and time again. Many organizations have chosen to use self-service technology systems that allow them to re-use catalog information in many different forms. These are based on content management systems that include the ability to syndicate the information content.

For these types of applications this apparently subtle difference is vital for the success of the system. By having this facility the same content can be re-purposed to integrate into the partner's system, even their own Website, without modifying the original data. Even more impressive, using XML technology the same content can be filtered for different language content, placement, and context. This is very important for any organization that is in the business of keeping this data up to date.

Other examples in this category include configuration management tools used to assist partners to determine whether what they are planning to order will be available and what the alternatives are. Generally, the most complex the product, or the more sophisticated the range of requirements, the greater the need for self-service systems. In recent months, the value of using e-learning tools and interactive collaboration systems to improve the way that an operation is running is also becoming a key differentiator in the development of CRM systems.

As firms understand that the development of CRM is often measured in terms of when the clients are exchanging money, rather than when interest and sign-up occurs. Distributed e-learning systems will help a company transfer knowledge to their customers very effectively, gaining important self-service ground from competitors.

Business intelligence

Successful CRM solutions are the result of a solid business strategy supported by technologies. By leveraging Internet technology, and combined with other systems, they often result in improvements in supply chain and other business processes. Analytics play an unsung (but crucial) role in this process: they enable organizations to monitor successes, failures, and all other intelligence regarding visitors and trans-actions on the site. In environments where complex and voluminous transactions are the norm, the metadata associated with these visitors is often more important than pure sales or revenue information alone. This data provides fundamental intelligence about what is happening in Web-based environments that will assist in the development and delivery of programs to improve customer service and account penetration using the Internet.

Where analytics and business intelligence matters

Analytics matters most in environments in e-marketplaces where buyers, sellers, and intermediaries gather to offer, sell, and buy products and services, facilitated by electronic means. One of the most widely known Internet sites, eBay, is an ideal example of a public e-marketplace. The human resources site Monster.com is another example. Public e-marketplaces are usually open to all comers and typically rely on some form of self-certification to permit transactions to take place.

In the business world, however, the bulk of transactions are conducted in private e-marketplaces. An e-marketplace does not necessarily have to be huge to warrant the use of these technologies. These private markets require qualified membership to participate. Differing levels of membership are defined by the business rules that govern the marketplace. For example, suppliers and providers may have different product offerings for different groups, discount levels, or international or taxation characteristics. These are all qualified during the sign-up process, which can take minutes if electronic qualification is possible (as on eBay) or may take longer if more due diligence is required for a particular membership status (as on the Cisco and IBM sites).

Public or private, each exchange defines a set of rules for bidding, trading, and fulfilling orders. In order to participate, buyers and sellers must agree to support these rules. Whether the goal is to buy product from IBM or Cisco, for example, or to bid on energy contracts at Altra.com, each participant is qualified before entering the marketplace. Some markets are hubs where multiple suppliers and buying agencies congregate (for example, Seafax.com for the fishing industry). Others represent dedicated sites where buyers can find specific services (such as Prosavvy.com for consultants).

The importance of analytics

Successful marketplaces and business Websites provide a service that the customer cannot do without. They connect clients with all the information, options, and resources to facilitate a transaction. Doing so requires electronic replication of many processes and a detailed understanding of how the product is relevant to the client. Making the connection to the right data elements is necessary for success.

Some back office applications, such as customer relationship management (CRM) systems, can serve up the necessary data. However, such applications may not always do the trick alone. Most of these applications focus on one part of the transaction, but not the impact of the entire business process.

Just as most companies today clearly understand the value of Web traffic analysis, CRM users need to understand what is happening inside their system to provide the next level of business improvement. They must analyze the vast quantities of data generated on these sites in order to understand their customers and to take actions based on that knowledge. They need to look at Web order trends, the relationship between products that are selling and Web traffic, cross-selling opportunities, promotions, and visitor demographics. This kind of analysis is particularly important for B2B e-marketplaces because:

» they have unusually high volumes of transactions;
» they often have high numbers of visitors;
» the business transactions are often more complex than those for electronic stores;
» members may have many differing profiles that need to be understood and interpreted;
» rapid changes in market conditions often require a rapid reflection in service offering at the exchange level; and
» most are tightly integrated with mission critical back office systems such as ERP, finance, and CRM solutions.

This need drives the increasing application of technology such as decision support systems, business intelligence tools, knowledge management applications, and data mining. And, as the demand increases, vendors are developing platforms that include such analytics.

They benefit from examining their business by a number of methods.

» Website analytics can reveal traffic volume and patterns, visitor paths, timeframes, purchases, where customers came from, where they went, what they liked, and what they disliked.

» Customer analytics reveal specific information regarding an individual or groups of customers.

Partner analytics show how partners behave when visiting the site.

» Revenue analytics show trends and patterns by market, product, region, demographics, and individuals.
» Performance analytics show how the site is performing and identify issues that could impact customer satisfaction.

All CRM analytics solutions, whether business-to-employee (B2E), B2B, or B2C, have to analyze what is happening on their sites and why. E-marketers have long understood the value of analytics. Most online marketing and sales campaigns vie for the same funding dollars as their non-Web counterparts. As a result, measuring and refining program success is vital. Marketers can quickly refine and improve their campaigns by tracking who enters the site, following visitor activities, and determining what visitors found interesting or dull.

The value of this information in specific applications (such as marketing) is clear. However, tackling such a project for an entire marketplace can be daunting. The volume of hits can be in the millions, the number of visitors in the tens of thousands, and the potential data sources extremely varied (for example, data sources can include CRM systems, intranets, extranets, and more). Decomposing this data into useful information requires sophisticated analysis tools.

> Knowledge management systems allow organizations to store, disseminate, exploit, and re-use corporate information and experience, with the goal of synthesizing knowledge to improve business operations.

In the B2E environment, knowledge management, and business intelligence tools have been deployed in large numbers for several years. These are now considered the baseline for most operations in order to create an environment for B2B and B2C systems to flourish. Now, applying analytics can produce competition-busting and productivity improvements in many ways. Examples of analytic applications and tools include:

» *ERP systems*: which enable improvements in inventory control, production processes, supply chain optimization, forward planning intelligence, contingency planning, and configuration management;

» *data mining*: for identification and creation of metadata, trends, organization of information in both structured and unstructured form, trend analysis, and classification of information not easily identified by other means;

» *knowledge management*: for self-service customer support applications, changes to products or services, changes to support procedures, decreasing cost of sale and service, and allowing internal and external users to gain access to relevant information quickly and easily;

» *CRM*: for personalization, customization, cross-selling, identifying trends, forecasting, competitive intelligence, and supplier relationship intelligence;

» *business intelligence*: for improved analysis of corporate data, delivering relevant information to employees, partners, and clients, extending information flow, and predicting behavior;

» *Web analysis*: for traffic patterns and volume, visitors, referrals, and content management;

» *marketing analysis*: for buying trends, branding, program measurement, on-line campaigns, self-service, market research, and campaign planning and management;

» *content management*: for personalization and customization trends, dynamic serving of content, syndication activities and management, and integration with e-marketing and self-service applications.

As organizations try to optimize their offerings, the more intelligence they can gather about the internal behavior of their own businesses and their interactions with partners and clients, the better. In an e-business, this data is particularly important. You can't "see" what others are doing in the marketplace without using analytics; therefore, you can't make targeted intelligence improvements.

Determining where best to use these tools and how to develop these systems is largely based on where business opportunities or problems lie. The lesson learned in the past two years of serious e-commerce on the Internet are the same as the ones from the client/server era: you need to understand how people are interacting with the systems in order to create improvements.

This understanding becomes even more important in the case of e-business activity. Because you can't see what others are doing in the "store" without analytics, it is impossible to make changes without the data. As many business and e-marketplaces become a hybrid of internal, external, and client-based systems, analytics will move from a "nice to have" to a "must have." Those without them will be driving with one headlight, without a high beam option.

In Practice: CRM Success Stories

What are the secrets of building a successful CRM system? This chapter explains how Ceridian, Toyota, Bose, and Singapore Cable Vision have managed to create some of the most successful CRM systems in the market today. It includes case studies of their systems.

CASE STUDIES

Building successful CRM solutions has not been an easy task. In an IT industry where more than 40% of all projects fail to make it to completion, CRM has had the recent distinction of a failure rate closer to 60%. Next to Enterprise Resource Planning systems, the failure of CRM solutions has been very visible. However, the benefits are still so huge (when the systems work) that it is worth taking the risk. We will examine three CRM case studies from different locations around the globe and see how they went about developing their solutions. As CRM is such a broad topic, and the needs of these organizations are so diverse, there is no "one size fits all" solution. These examples are used to show how some successful implementations have been developed and deployed. They are not endorsements of the specific vendors' products. As there are literally hundreds of software vendors providing various solutions in the marketplace, it would be hard to cover this ground adequately within the confines of this short book.

NORTH AMERICA

Based in Winnipeg, Manitoba, Ceridian Canada is that country's leading provider of payroll and human resource management services, effectively processing one of every six paychecks. As the competition among service providers has intensified, the need to provide top-quality customer service became Ceridian Canada's primary strategic goal. Recognizing this, the company reengineered its core customer service processes around a team-based model, while at the same time it created an information processing infrastructure – specifically CRM and Web-based self-service – to achieve these goals.

By providing company-wide access to a unified customer database, Ceridian Canada's new "STAR" platform allows the company to move from branch level customer care processes to a nationwide "virtual call center" model.

Ceridian Canada selected Siebel's CRM solution to power its new customer service platform (known as STAR), and chose IBM WebSphere Application Server as the foundation of a new customer self-service solution. IBM Global Services was instrumental in nearly all phases of

Ceridian Canada's initiative, from planning and design to implementation and training.

Core functionality

Ceridian Canada's CRM solution allows its newly deployed account management teams (which replaced individual account reps) to access a single national database of customer information, which provides a full profile of each customer's account history. A built-in knowledge management capability allows for faster resolution and less frequent escalation. The Web self-service solution, now in beta, will allow customers to access (and in some cases update or modify) their account information via a browser.

Like many outsourced services, the Canadian market for payroll processing services has in recent years undergone significant consolidation. In a market that once supported nearly half a dozen significant competitors, Ceridian Canada and ADP Canada (a unit of US-based ADP Corporation) have emerged as dominant players. As the market has evolved, underlying product line has assumed less importance as a competitive differentiator, reflecting the commodity or "utility" status that characterizes payroll service offerings today. At the same time, quality customer service – already a key strategic competency – has emerged as the industry's pivotal competitive requirement. Payroll providers have addressed the customer service issue on two levels. In addition to focusing on standard customer service metrics – such as problem resolution timeframes – providers are seeking to improve customer satisfaction by providing alternative service delivery channels, such as Web-based self-service.

Having emerged from two companies, Ceridian Canada faced the challenges of unifying a fragmented, often divergent, set of business processes. Foremost among these was customer service. While cultural factors represented a significant barrier to the implementation of common customer service practices, structural factors – such as a high degree of geographic dispersion – made synchronization even harder. According to Mark Alpern, vice president of customer care and quality, the prevailing "branch-centric" approach to customer interaction made the construction of a consistent set of processes very difficult. "Under our previous framework, customer information for the

Winnipeg branch was held in Winnipeg, the Halifax branch was held in Halifax, and so on," says Alpern. "There was a lack of consistency in process from branch to branch to the extent that each branch was unique." Ceridian Canada's disparate IT infrastructure – another vestige of its formation – further exacerbated the problem.

In addition to fragmented information resources, the company's generic customer service approach, based on account management, was also emerging as a point of vulnerability. Under this approach, each account manager would be responsible for servicing as many as 150 customers. However, as the company grew it became clear that the individualized approach to customer service would have to be modified to ensure continued success into the future. Feedback from customer surveys validated what Ceridian management had come to know: customers were becoming increasingly frustrated at not being able to reach their service rep by phone on the first try. By 1999, the need to reengineer Ceridian Canada's fundamental approach to customer service was clear.

The company responded swiftly, redesigning its customer service processes around a team-based structure, which allowed a customer's inquiry to be addressed by various members of an account team. For customers, the benefits of this team-based approach were manifold – greatly improved access, faster problem resolution, and generally higher satisfaction. But for Ceridian, the move to a team-based customer service model also required a more flexible, integrated infrastructure for sharing data within the company. As Alpern explains, the company's "change in philosophy" on customer service required an equally bold initiative on the technology side. "We saw the need to fundamentally change the way we store, access, and use customer information," says Alpern. "This in turn required a shift in our infrastructure strategy towards a more centralized, standardized approach."

Ceridian Canada's redefined approach to customer service and customer data management rested on two key technological pillars. First was the company's decision to implement a CRM solution company-wide that would provide the main point of entry for account teams servicing customers. The second element – underpinning this – would be the creation of a single national customer database to replace branch-specific customer information databases.

In addition to focusing its e-business initiatives on employees (e.g., using CRM to facilitate team-based customer service), the company has also developed customer-facing Web-based solutions such as Powerpay, a fully Web-based payroll solution targeted to small businesses. While Powerpay represents a new element of Ceridian's core service portfolio, the company has also leveraged Web technology to expand its customer service delivery channels. The most important initiative in this area has centered around Web-based self-service, under which Ceridian Canada customers access various service features via a Web browser. In late 2000, the company examined the opportunity to leverage its CRM investments – the most crucial element of which was its national customer database. As conceived by Ceridian Canada, this solution would provide Web-based access to customer data drawn from the core CRM customer database. Moreover, like the CRM initiative from which it was derived, the Web self-service initiative was designed to improve the quality of customer service through increased convenience. Equally important, the platform was also seen as a scalable, low-cost channel for handling less complex customer inquiries.

One of the key technical challenges of the CRM project was the inherent complexity of the configuration effort, with the issue of legacy integration emerging as the single most important issue. As Aldridge explains, the fact that Ceridian Canada's branches had independently developed their own methods of gathering and storing data led to a proliferation of data formats. "Transferring data stored in multiple formats – stored on heterogeneous systems – to a single, standardized database proved to be a huge task," says Aldridge. "It serves to underscore the complexity of the problems that we originally set out to solve."

The pilot version of Ceridian Canada's Web self-service application began in March 2001, after a two-month development effort. The first phase of development focused on database integration, while the second focused on the user interface component of the solution. Since then, a beta version of the solution has been used by a limited number of customers. As Aldridge points out, the goals were twofold. "First, we wanted to create a functional application that could be tested by customers to ensure that it was what they wanted," relates Aldridge. "We also wanted to gain an understanding of the impact of the solution on existing internal processes and staffing requirements." Ultimately, Ceridian Canada plans to roll out the solution to all its customers – albeit using a gradual, phased approach that will allow them to gauge more accurately their infrastructure requirements.

Ceridian Canada's CRM solution – known internally as STAR (Service and Technology Achieving Results) – is used primarily by employees (customer care representatives and managers within the customer service organization). Other Ceridian users include billing and finance staff, who access STAR data through workflow from the customer care organization. The core of the STAR system is a centralized database that stores payroll account information, as well as a complete record of interaction between Ceridian Canada and the customer (telephone calls, faxes, and e-mail). Another important capability of the STAR system is its ability to create and track service requests when a live representative cannot address a customer's problem immediately. This workflow-like capability then allows the representative to identify the appropriate staff to address the inquiry. One of the STAR system's defining strengths is its integration with Ceridian Canada's core legacy systems. For example, if an employee using the STAR system makes a change to a customer's account information, that change is automatically fed into the company's payroll processing system (which handle all of Ceridian's mission-critical processes).

Ceridian Canada's national customer database – the core of the STAR solution – resides on the production database server. Data stored therein ranges from simple name, address, and contact information to production schedules (i.e., when customers run their payroll) to billing and remittance information (i.e., tax payments to government agencies). The STAR database is integrated with Ceridian Canada's various legacy systems – principally client/server systems – throughout the company's branches. The data flow between the STAR system and Ceridian Canada's legacy systems is bi-directional. For example, if an employee changes a customer's delivery address, that change would be propagated from the STAR system to Ceridian Canada's production system (controlling the addressing and mailing of checks). By the same token, data from the company's backend systems (e.g., billing) is uploaded to the STAR database on a batch basis.

Ceridian Canada expects the benefits of its recent e-business initiatives to show up in the metrics it values most – customer satisfaction and retention. In the intensely competitive payroll services market – where quality customer service is the key differentiator – customer satisfaction is perhaps the single most important benchmark of the company's well-being.[1]

BOSE

Bose Corporation is a respected name in sound and their equipment can be found in venues around the world. The field sales organization within Bose consists of regional sales groups with more than 200 individuals supporting an extensive reseller network. To do their jobs effectively, the sales representatives must interact and share information with many departments, including other sales groups, marketing, and customer service.

Historically, communication consisted of conference calls and call reports. Bose had now grown to the point where management realized that, in addition to being time-consuming and inefficient, this method of communication did not provide a means of measuring their cost of sales – an increasingly important objective. In its quest to create a more effective and efficient organization, Bose selected Siebel Systems for its e-business applications, and turned to Akibia to tailor the eCRM solution to meet their needs.

Akibia created a multi-phased solution that allowed Bose to quickly capture a return on their investment and continue to expand and add functionality as needed. Akibia's first goal was to build a foundation for sales management functions as well as addressing the needs of the field sales organization. Bose customers are resellers, including large retailers such as Circuit City. To effectively manage their customers, the field sales group needed a way to plan, track, and manage their own field activities and have access to the corporate promotions that Bose was offering to resellers. In addition, the solution enabled lead tracking functions for the groups who deal directly with phone calls from potential customers.

Akibia began working on this first phase in March 2000 and by September had rolled out the solution to 220 users within the Bose sales organization. The second phase provided additional function-ality for various groups, most notably the account management team. The solution allows the Bose field service organization to use the eCRM system to work strategically with their customers, creating busi-ness plans and tailored programs for each customer. In addition, the field sales managers can track and manage dealer/reseller promotions through the eCRM system, including promotional funds and inventory records of product displays. The system also allows all users of the system to track and submit time and expenses.

Tim Arnold, manager, e-business strategy at Bose Corporation, explains:

> "With our field service organization, we have hundreds of people spread throughout the country working on thousands of activities at any given time.
>
> Part of the challenge in implementing an eCRM solution in this environment is that you're not able to see and work with the sales organization on a daily basis to understand all of what they do. To create a solution that addresses all of their needs and the company's needs, and to get the sales organization to 'buy in' to the solution, you really need their input and feedback. Akibia helped with this process by going in to our regional sales offices, soliciting input and giving the sales force ownership in the process.
>
> When we were ready for rollout, training was provided to each group, ensuring that the system would be used to the fullest."

For Bose, the result of their eCRM implementation has been a more efficient and effective field sales organization. But this is just the first step of a corporate commitment to eCRM. "The growth of e-commerce, combined with having multiple sales channels, have the potential to cause conflict among our sales channels and impact customer service," said Arnold. "Bose as a company is dedicated to creating experiences for our customers that are enlightening, unique and delightful. But you can only 'delight' your customers to the extent that you 'delight' your channel partners as well. We see eCRM as the tool that will enable us to do this and Akibia is our partner in helping to manage and expand the application throughout the company."

SINGAPORE CABLE VISION

As far back as 1994, Singapore Cable Vision Ltd (SCV) understood the opportunities for new business and services as the broadcast, information technology, and telecommunications industries converged. In 1999, SCV completed construction of its entire broadband network – three months ahead of schedule.

SCV currently employs more than 800 people and provides two broadband services: SCV MaxTV, its multi-channel cable TV service, to which 260,000 homes subscribe; and SCV MaxOnline, the broadband Internet access service via cable modem, currently used in over 42,000 homes.

SCV's director of operations, James Woo, realized that transforming SCV from a product-centric business to a customer-centric one was crucial to SCV's survival. He also knew that establishing CRM in the customer service center was a logical place to start. "The call center had little notes posted all over the place, with information about customers and the reasons for calling them back. Sometimes, when the customer service operator (CSO) was busy, requests would sometimes go unfulfilled," says Woo.

Woo also wanted to capture information about potential customers who inquired but did not immediately purchase services. The little notes that the CSOs used could not adequately capture this vital information.

Long response time to customers' requests was another problem. "Most of the time, when customers had some issues with the service, they called up the CSO or even sent a letter. Because of this, the other departments did not have any form of ownership of these issues," explains Woo.

Woo knew that the customer service department was not solely responsible for solving all of these problems. "The service of our customers is not just a responsibility of the customer service depart-ment, rather the whole company. That was why we were looking at CRM products in the first place."

Woo wanted to set up user-friendly CRM using the latest proven technologies to capture customer transactions. The system also had to send incidents to the multiple departments, plus interface with the legacy billing system. He chose Onyx Employee Portal-Windows

Client to provide customer-facing teams with a comprehensive tool for managing, sharing, and viewing all customer information, with plans to deploy the solution in other vital departments; plus a knowledge base to supply access to information across the organization via the Internet. SCV carried out the implementation with two consultants from Onyx. The solution is built on a Windows NT cluster that is linked to the CSOs via independent terminals.

In each of these cases, the clients have had success with the systems they deployed not just because it was built on solid technology foundations, but because they linked business goals, work process change, and the technology in a common framework. The goals that have been achieved by these systems include:

» much improved response time to customers queries and requests;
» knowledge capture as customers interact with the systems, call center operators, or CSOs;
» improved accountability and measurability of the customer relationship;
» development of Internet-ready systems to permit self-service and personal service aspects of the system;
» reduced costs of sales and support;
» lower administration costs; and
» increased staff efficiency.

NOTE

1 Case study courtesy IBM Corporation.

Key Concepts and Thinkers

CRM has its own language. Get to grips with the lexicon of CRM through the *Express Exec* branding glossary in this chapter, which also covers:

» key concepts, including Patricia Seybold;
» an A-Z of terms and glossary.

PATRICIA SEYBOLD

Many might argue that Patti Seybold has forgotten more about CRM than we may ever learn. Her detailed studies concerning what works for many firms have become well known around the world. Her latest research is clearly documented in her latest book (with Ronni Marshak), *The Customer Revolution*.[1] She has developed an eight-step process to help measure customer value, monitor experiences, and ensure they can give a great customer experience to their own clients.

Step 1: Create a compelling brand experience

Ensuring that your brand leaves the impression that you are the *one* that the client really wants to do business with, is critical to any customer success. In *The Customer Revolution*, Seybold provides examples of how companies can create an exciting but differentiated experience to position their brand correctly in the marketplace.

Step 2: Deliver a seamless experience across channels and touchpoints

Today's customers are demanding that companies offer them convenience and freedom of choice. Customers want to decide where they will place an order, visit a store, make a telephone call or order on the Internet. They want a seamless experience across channels and touchpoints, and expect the same level of service and support regardless of whether they shop on-line, via catalog, or at a bricks-and-mortar store.

The term "touchpoint" describes the type of media through which customers interact with companies. Touchpoints are stores, telephones, mail, fax, kiosks, and the Web. Customers choose which touchpoint to use depending on things like location, preference, and the time of day. For example, a customer could order a computer over the Internet or by visiting a retailer.

For those firms that sell across channels, the success of relationships with channel partners, particularly if you are both selling to the same client base, is key. While many dealers and retailers are intent on owning their relationships with customers, many of those same customers desire access to alternative channels and look to the manufacturer to provide them directly. Careful management of channel conflict is rapidly become a core strategic skill, required for the multi-level distribution models in the market today.

Step 3: Care about customers and their outcomes

The companies that can thrive in the customer economy are those that have a corporate culture and set of core values centered around caring about customers – not just as revenue targets, profit contributors, or advertising magnets, but as people. Customer loyalty and lifetime customer value are two key metrics that foreshadow success in the customer economy. One is totally linked to the other.

Lids is a company that understands what its customers want, and delivers. Lids was started by two college students in 1991 who noticed that the hip student uniform included baseball caps, but heard complaints about how hard it was to find those caps. Today, the company has over 500 retail outlets and a thriving Internet business.

At first, small stores were placed in malls, where the target market, males between 12 and 24 years old, gathered. Lids offered a one-stop shop for a wide variety of baseball caps. What wasn't in stock could be ordered and either delivered to the buyer's home or the store for pick-up.

During 1998, Lids started a Web store. They made a special cash card available, and merged the inventory management so everything was available on-line. The card could be used in the store or on-line. With the database tracking, purchases could be tracked in either location. They started a special program called HeadFirst™ which rewarded repeat buyers with one hat for every five they bought. The program was a tremendous success, with the average HeadFirst client buying 7.5 hats per year.

Step 4: Measure what matters to customers

Most companies measure and monitor sales and profits, customer growth and defection, inventory turns and profit margins. If they have a Website, they also measure hits and clicks, unique visitors, and abandoned carts. But none of these metrics matter to our customers. The companies that will be pulling ahead over the next few years are those that take the quality of their customers' experience very seriously. They cannot measure what is a good experience for you, although they will tell you what is, one way or the other. To compete with the best in the industry it is important to access the entire quality of the experience of doing business with you, either directly or through your partner channel. Seybold makes the case for designing your business around the outcomes that are important to your customers. Here are some suggestions.

» Measure what is important to customers.
» Make a list of the common tasks customers have.
» Find out how easy it is to do business with your company.
» Track the time it takes to interact and respond to a client.
» Send out "mystery shoppers" to test the experience of dealing with your firm. Get them to rate the experience.

Step 5: Hone operational excellence

Having understood what the issues are for your client and customer, start working on fixing the problem. By honing operational excellence, many things can be improved inside the organization. One recommendation is to design a back-end process for a new service before it is introduced to the client.

Step 6: Value customers' time

Very few things are higher up the annoyance list for clients than wasting their time. Just as the earlier experience with Chrysler illustrates (see Chapter 2), firms that focus on making good use of their clients' time will flourish in a customer-centric economy. To avoid problems:

» streamline decision-making;
» offer ubiquitous, convenient access; and
» design processes using customer scenarios.

To improve customer decision-making, provide the information customers need to make a decision. For example, if you have a Web-based search engine, permit searches by key word, category, or model. Offer side-by-side comparisons, photographs, and illustrations. Google is a great example, where searches can be made by image as well as keyword. Inform customers about delivery methods and timeframes.

Educate clients about installation and troubleshooting data. Make it easy for clients to get hold of someone who can help, even if it means offering service 24 hours a day.

Step 7: Place customer DNA at the core

A great way to improve customer loyalty is to simplify customers' lives by managing issues they think are important. Customers are more willing to use Web self-service applications to manage parts of their lives, for example, banking, digital photography, and college savings. Many business clients now want and demand the management of inventory, purchasing, and supply chain information to all be available on-line.

As biological DNA controls the body's processes, our *customer* DNA should attract the right services, in the right context, at the right time. If your car requires a service, an appointment should be offered and scheduled. If inventory needs replenishment, approved suppliers and logistics partners should take action to provide you with your needs.

Step 8: Design to morph

In this final step, Seybold gets us ready for change, the change we have to deal with every day of the week. Whether we need to change our business model four times a year may be a stretch, but there is certainly a need to do it several times in the current market turmoil. Here are some pointers she gives as to when we should look for change.

» It feels right. Trust your intuition. There's no business logic or market research that can rival human intuition.
» Your customers give you clues. When customers begin asking for new services – listen.
» Prospects give you clues. Listen when prospects ask you if you could offer a particular service.
» Existing partners want you to provide a service for them. Sometimes partners ask for special services that may make their partnering easy. Listen to them. You may be able to provide a service and collect a fee.
» You know you are onto something but haven't quite got it right. Experiment with initiatives until you have the product or service

offering correct. Do not be afraid to offer several alternatives until you find out which one will be the winner.

» The market is moving away from your business model. In order to stay on top of market trends, be diligent about bringing in new customers who may not look and act like your old customers.

» Your business model is still evolving, sometimes attracting a market niche you weren't targeting in your initial business plan. Markets move fast, keep an open mind about what will and will not work.

A – Z OF CRM TERMS AND THINKING

The following is a guide to terms and technologies that are mentioned frequently in relation to CRM systems and how they are deployed.

Application Server – A computer in an intranet/Internet environment that performs the data processing necessary to deliver up-to-date information as well as process information for Web clients. The application server resides with/or between the Web server and the databases and legacy applications, providing the middleware glue to enable a browser-based application to link to multiple sources of information.

Authentication – The name of the process of verifying the identity of a user as they log onto a network.

Bandwidth – The amount of data that can travel through a communications network (such as the Internet) in a specific period of time. This is usually measured in seconds.

Berners-Lee, Tim – While working in Geneva, Switzerland at CERN, the European Particle Physics Laboratory, Berners-Lee created the World Wide Web.

Brochureware – The act of putting your corporate literature in basic static form directly onto a Website. Often bores visitors to death, and causes rapid exits from the site.

Bulletin Board System – Often referred to as a BBS, this system allows others to read, comment, and electronically post new messages to the group reading them. Often used for interest groups, customer support, or professional groups, BBS systems represent a low cost and effective collaboration forum for the Internet.

Channels of distribution – A distribution channel is a method of providing your product or service to the target user of the system.

This could be an on-line mall, portal, your own brand site, or distribution supply chain.

Change management – The program to define, implement, and refine the changes required for the business to affect a change in strategy, process and technology. Used extensively in existing bricks-and-mortar firms to assist staff to transition to new business practices.

Clicks-and-mortar – Organizations that have bricks-and-mortar (traditional non-Internet based businesses) that have changed their strategies to provide both on-line and off-line channels for their clients and business partners.

Click-thru – The act of clicking (with a mouse) on a particular graphic or element on a Web page. These are measured to determine the effectiveness of advertising, content, and traffic patterns of individual Websites.

Closed loop lead management – The process of qualifying, distributing, managing, and measuring sales leads inside a CRM. An effective closed loop lead management system should yield measurements that indicate overall marketing program effectiveness, lead closure rates, competitive information from the sales engagement, product requirements, sales efficiency, forecasting, and funnel reports for sales on status and stages of leads awaiting closure.

Community – Electronic forum where individuals and groups gather to find relevant and pertinent information. They are often segmented by interest or geography.

Content management – The system and method by which content is updated, changed, and re-posted to the Website.

Cookie – File that stores a user's personal preferences for Internet information and communication tools in memory while the browser is running. In addition to personal preferences, cookies can also save information such as the date that the Website was visited, what purchases were made, what ad banners were clicked on, what files were downloaded, and the information viewed.

CPM – Cost per thousand impressions. A measurement of how many times someone has viewed your banner ad via a browser.

Customer Relationship Management – Technology systems and internal processes to support the continuous relationship with clients from early stage prospecting through to customer support.

Typically provide support for sales, marketing, support, finance, and increasingly workflow processes to allow clients to serve themselves with information and product.

Disintermediation - Being excluded from a business network or supply chain due to new market conditions, pricing, or distribution process and operations. Usually happens when the value being provided by the organization is not high enough to prevent getting squeezed out of the chain.

Early adopters - Groups of users and individuals that will typically adopt technology and new work processes early in their introduction to the marketplace.

EDI - Electronic Data Interchange. The controlled transfer of data between businesses and organizations via established security standards.

Extranets - Private WANs (see below) that run on public protocols with the goal of fostering collaboration and information sharing between organizations. A feature of extranets is that companies can allow certain guests to have access to internal data on a controlled basis.

E-tailing - On-line sales of retail style goods.

E-zine - On-line publications in the form of newsletters or magazines that are allow for a new way for communication and interaction to occur on the Internet e.g. http://www.salon.com.

FAQ (Frequently Asked Questions) - Helpful way for new users to look at questions that are regularly asked, usually saved on a bulletin board or as archived files.

File server - A computer that stores and makes available programs and data available to other computers on a connected network.

Firewall - A software/hardware combination that separates an internal local area network from the external Internet. This is done for security purposes in order to protect a company's network from the outside world and unauthorized electronic visitors.

Gateway - A hardware or software component that links two otherwise incompatible applications or networks.

Impressions - Each occasion that an element of a page has been viewed by an individual browser. Often used to count Internet ad placements.

Intranet - Internet-based computing networks that are private and secure. Typically used by corporations, government, and other organizations, these are based upon Internet standards and provide the means for an organization to make resources more readily available to its employees on-line.

Java – A programming language that was created in 1995 in order to allow Java programs to be downloaded and run on a Web browser. Developed by Sun Microsystems, Java is an object-oriented programming language that allows content and software to be distributed through the Internet. Applications that are written in Java must be run by a Java-enabled Web browser.

Killer app (application) – An incredibly useful, creative program that provides a breakthrough for its users. The first killer app of the Internet was e-mail.

LAN (Local Area Network) – A computer network that operates and is located in one specific location. Many of these may be connected together in order to enable users to share resources and information on their network.

Legacy systems – Generally described as an existing computer system that is providing a function for some part of the business. These systems are considered older in nature, but often provide some strategic function to the business. Examples include:

» inventory management systems;
» Manufacturing Resource Planning systems (MRP);
» Enterprise Resource Planning (ERP);
» sales automation systems;
» helpdesk systems.

MIME – Multipurpose Internet Mail Extension, a standard method to identify the type of data contained in a file based on its extension. MIME is an Internet protocol that allows you to send binary files across the Internet as attachments to e-mail messages. These files includes graphics, programs, sound, and video files, as well as electronic office files. MIME allows different types of systems to interpret these different file types successfully.

Mirroring – Exact copying of the content of one computer disk to another. Used to back up information in mission critical systems, and permit the maintenance of others while the system is still running.

Moore's Law – Gordon E. Moore, co-founder of Intel, said in 1965 that he predicted that the processing power of integrated circuits would double every 18 months for the next 10 years. This law has proven true for almost 30 years and is now used in many performance forecasts. Moore's second law is that the cost of production would double every generation.

Newsgroup – An electronic discussion group comprising of collections of postings to particular topics. These topics are posted to a server designated as the news server for this group. Newsgroups can be an invaluable source of information and advice when trying to resolve problems and get advice.

Newsreader – A software program that lets you subscribe to newsgroups, in addition to reading and posting messages to them. Will keep track of groups visited and favorites for simplified navigation when returning and tracking activities in different groups.

Netiquette – Set of rules users are encouraged to follow if participating in an electronic discussion group or sending e-mail on the Internet.

NIH – Not Invented Here.

One-to-one marketing – Customization and personalization of both product and prospect requirements to meet an individual set of established needs. Once matched, a one-to-one marketing program delivers an exact marketing message, with the appropriate product to meet the prospect's needs.

Personalization – Customization of web information to specifically meet the needs and desires of the individual user.

Portal – Major visiting center for Internet users. The very large portals started life as search engines. AltaVista, AOL, CompuServe, Excite, Infoseek, Lycos, Magellan, and Yahoo! are examples of major portals. B2B portals offer locations for individual business transactions to occur specific to affinity groups and business needs.

Redirectors – Programs that send visitors of one segment of a web site to a new location automatically.

Replication – Describes the process of controlled copying of certain elements of a Website, database, or other collection of information. A technique that can provide portions of a system to be automatically distributed to the area that needs it for performance or other reasons.

Robot – A robot is a program that is designed to automatically go out and explore the Internet for a specific purpose. Some robots record and index all of the contents of the network to create searchable database. Such robots are called spiders.

Router – A system at the intersection of two networks that works to determine which path is most efficient for data when traveling to its destination.

Server – A software program that functions in a client-server information exchange model whose function is to provide information and execute functions for a computer attached to the network.

Shareware – Software that is made available to users, by the developers, at no cost. Manufacturers of shareware often ask users to review the applications and sometimes request a fee of $10–$25. Shareware is available on Websites, such as www.jumbo.com, www.shareware.com, and www.tucows.com.

Spam – The practice of sending e-mail or posting messages for purely commercial gain, often to very large groups of uninterested users.

Spoofing – Slang for someone impersonating another on the Internet. Typically used in electronic mail applications.

Stickiness – A general term to describe the characteristics of a Website that attract and keep users. Also a measurement of how many users return to the site for more information or products.

Supply chain management – The management of materials, information, and finances as they move through the process from supplier to manufacturer to wholesaler to retailer to consumer with the goal of optimizing development and delivery of products and services.

Targeted marketing – Development of marketing programs by identifying segments in specific markets and designing the product or service to specifically meet these needs.

Templates – Pre-defined application components that allow rapid development and deployment of computer-based systems.

URLs (Uniform Resource Locators) – The standard form for addresses on the Internet that provide the addressing system for other Internet locations.

Virtual Private Networks – Private networks that allow users to purchase bandwidth and access, often through their Internet connection, without the need to purchase dedicated network cabling or systems.

Wallets – Electronic wallets offer the ability for shoppers on the Internet to automatically debit their accounts using e-money. The wallet contains electronic money which is usually deposited in advance, and is replenished as the account needs it. This is likely to become a more common form of shopping in the future.

WAN (Wide Area Network) – Made up of local networks that are connected to other local networks by high-speed telephone lines.

Whiteboard – The electronic equivalent to a chalkboard, whiteboards provide visual communication and interaction over networks.

Wired – Term used to describe users who are attached to their computers or use the computer and the Web as in integral part of their lifestyle.

World Wide Web – A collection of protocols and standards that make it possible to view and retrieve information from the Internet. By being linked together in a hypermedia system, this information can be used through the World Wide Web.

WYSIWYG (What You See Is What You Get) – Term used to refer to text and graphics that will print in the same format that it is seen on the screen.

XML – Extensible Markup Language describes the structure of, and provides application control over the content of, the documents and systems using this language. Much more powerful than HTML, XML is likely to be the next generation language for the Web and business applications.

NOTE

1 Seybold, P.B. & Marshak, R. (2001) *The Customer Revolution*. Crown Publishing, New York.

Resources

Much has been written on the subject of CRM. This chapter identifies the best resources:

» Websites;
» books and articles on CRM.

CRM

Recommended reading

» Evans, P & Wurster, T.S. (2000) *Blown to Bits*. Harvard Business School Press, Boston.
» Hagel, J. & Armstrong, A.G. (1997) *Net Gain*. Harvard Business School Press, Boston.
» Hagel, J. & Singer, M. (1999) *Net Worth*. Harvard Business School Press.
» Harry, M. & Schroeder, R. (2000) *Six Sigma*. Random House, New York.
» Haylock, C.F. & Muscarella, L. (1999) *NetSuccess*. Adams Media Corporation, Avon, MA.
» Kaplan, R. & Norton, D.P. (2001) *The Strategy Focused Organization*. Harvard Business School Press, Boston.
» Meyer, C. & Davis, S. (1998) *Blur: The Speed of Change in the Connected Economy*. Capstone, London.
» Miller, W. (1998) *Flash of Brilliance*. Perseus Books, Reading, MA.
» Moore, G. (1995) *Inside the Tornado*. HarperBusiness, New York.
» Neuhauser, P. Bender, R. & Stromberg, K. (2000) *Culture.com*. John Wiley and Sons, New York.
» Peppers and Rogers (1997) *Enterprise One to One*. DoubleDay, New York.
» Segil, L. (2001) *Fast Alliances*. Wiley, New York.
» Senge, P.M. (1990) *The Fifth Discipline*. DoubleDay, New York.
» Seybold, P.B. (1998) *Customers.Com*. Random House, New York.
» Seybold, P.B. & Marshak, R. (2001) *The Customer Revolution*. Crown Publishing, New York.
» Siebel, T.M. (1999) *Cyber Rules: Strategies for Excelling at E-Business*. Doubleday, New York.

In addition to these book resources, some excellent resources for specific topics are listed below. These will provide up-to-date information on particular CRM areas that are changing and evolving rapidly.

The following are excellent Web-based resources for e-marketing activities.

eMA – eMarketing Association

The eMA is a professional organization for companies and individuals involved in the practice of e-marketing and the integration of on-line and off-line marketing activities. This site provides resources such as white papers, newsletters, Web tools, and articles, as well as information about professional certifications.

» http://www.emarketingassociation.com

Wilson Internet – Web marketing & e-commerce

This site, created by Ralph F. Wilson, is one of the best free sources for e-marketing resources on the Web. The site includes a large collection of free articles, a newsletter, and recommended books, all highlighting e-marketing best practices. This is a great resource for firms currently using the Internet as a key component of overall marketing strategy.

» http://www.wilsonweb.com/

Brint.com – e-business

Brint.com has long been recognized as an excellent resource for business professionals. The site includes a section devoted to e-business in which many relevant topics are covered, including a directory of Web marketing resources.

» http://www.ebiztechnet.com/cgi-bin/links/links.pl?passurl = /Computers/Internet/Marketing/Resources/

PORTALS

Techtarget.com

Hosts a special section on their web site specifically for CRM applications. Lots in introductory material, right through to vendor benchmarking and case studies. A mine of information.

ZDnet.com

High profile infomediary with a good CRM section. Search for relevant articles and product reviews.

CIO.com

This site bills itself as "The Leading Resource for Information Executives." Topics covered by CIO.com are organized into knowledge centers. Although there is not a specific knowledge center for portals, a search for "portal" will turn up hundreds of articles on the subject.

» www.cio.com

Intranet Journal

The Intranet Journal is an excellent source for information on portals as well as other technology utilized by intranets. The site offers access to articles and case studies as well as an Intranet Events Calendar.

» http://www.intranetjournal.com

CRM

The following are excellent Web-based resources for CRM activities.

» http://www.callcenterexchange.com.
» http://www.CallCenterOps.com – Information for those who are involved in customer service via a call center or help desk.
» http://www.CallCenterWorld.com.
» http://www.CRMAssist.com (IT Toolbox) – A communication and collaboration tool for collective groups of IT and business professionals to solve problems related to purchasing, implementation, and support.
» http://www.CRMCommunity.com.
» http://www.CRM-Forum.com – Provides CRM professionals and companies involved in CRM on both the demand and supply side of the industry with a place to keep up to date with CRM developments, and to meet, discuss, and contact each other about CRM-related issues.
» InformationWeek on CRM: http://www.informationweek.com/techcenters/sw/bizapps/crm.

» Peppers and Rogers Group: http://www.1to1.com/Building/CustomerRelationships/entry.jsp – The Peppers and Rogers corporate portfolio includes thought leadership and strategic consulting services, designed to increase customer loyalty and satisfaction while increasing profitability.

Ten Steps to Making CRM Work

Building a successful CRM solution requires a plan of action. This final chapter provides some key insights into creating and implementing a CRM solution in today's business environment, covering the following steps.

- » Building a Customer Ready Organization (CRO)
- » Vision
- » Values
- » Opportunity analysis
- » The framework
- » Planning
- » Research and preparation
- » Implementation
- » CRM
- » The Knowledge Management System
- » Back office.

BUILDING A CUSTOMER READY ORGANIZATION (CRO)

The powerful bonds that exist between trust, technology, customers, and work practices have never been more prized, nor more valued. Our earlier chapters have identified the need and the building importance of an effective CRM foundation system to begin the process. The Customer Ready Organization is ready to do business with many organizations. Their partners, consumers, other businesses, operate within a supply chain and in other marketplaces. They are ready to optimize the way they want to operate, and have the need, attitude, technology, and work processes to support many differing relationships. CRO firms understand the power of relationships and how to work them.

The development of the CRO strategy is not a simple process. With so many things to consider, the easy way out is often selected first. We have to look at the corporation and its goals in holistic manner. Values, vision, goals, partnerships processes, and customers all form part of the continuum. Organizations that have been very effective in building multidimensional customer strategies have one very important thing in common. They all keep their values and vision aligned, in fact the values are more important than the vision in the development of effective partnerships.

By linking values and vision, an organization keeps the critical elements in the same frame. The reason values are critical is that they affect the behavior of the organization. The B2E system we discussed earlier will provide the basic foundation for any CRO or company. Winning ways are to be found in every organization that has followed the strategy. Microsoft, Sun Microsystems, Vignette, and WorldCom have all used a powerful CRM system as the basis for their strategies.

VIVA!

Linking **VI**sion and **VA**lues is an outstanding starting place for the organization. Alignment of vision and values creates an overlap that will bootstrap almost any partnership initiative. The vision is the direction of the company and the values are the guidelines used to reach the destination. One is the engine, the other is the wheels.

1. VISION

Ensuring that the company is following its vision may seem like an obvious point in the development of CRM strategies. However, it is sometimes overlooked. Vision provides the guidance for where the firm is going, the spotlight highlighting the target. Visions can be built around some future goal that supports the premise of the organization (its product or mission) or can be more of a statement of desired self-perception.

Vision statements come in all shapes and sizes. Sometimes these vision statements are focused purely on the partnership issue. Others are based on the global strategy of the organization. There is no right or wrong in either approach.

2. VALUES

Values are tightly linked to customers because they control the way an organization considers change, deals with others, and the quality of the results. For example, in the consulting business, particularly strategic consulting, moving to a position of trusted adviser to the client is paramount. To reach a position of trusted adviser means applying values in the business such as quality, honesty, integrity, and performance. These values have to be practiced day after day in the organization, and they have to be reconciled with individual departmental goals and metrics.

A fellow board member once told me, "There has to be a short term in order to have a long term." While in financial terms this is true, in value terms it expresses the danger short- and medium-term goals can have on a value statement. If the short term requires "making the numbers" at any cost, firms can find themselves taking business they cannot fulfill effectively or, worse still, opening the door to problems of quality and customer service. We have all found sales staff that will try and sell regardless of the product and the need to the client. But this is not the profile of a long-term success in the sales profession. Values rate highly for those that want the long-term relationship. The short-term sale or the short-term client could be expensive in more ways than one.

Using VIVA as a method of creating a link between values and vision can also identify potential problems in the process. VIVA is all about linking the vision and values in a common framework. Blockers at a high level can be identified early in the process.

3. OPPORTUNITY ANALYSIS

If you have a latent desire to build a CRO strategy, finding the starting point is the first stop on the way. Before reviewing the rest of the framework and programs needed to implement these systems, an analysis of why you should proceed needs to be conducted. This will effectively measure the goal of the partnership opportunity early in the process, and then provide some guidelines for how to advance.

An opportunity analysis is a good tool to use in this process. This process will allow you to determine the reasons and metrics that you will use to measure the effectiveness. While the author obviously supports the development of partner relationships, I also recognize that most partnerships fail to meet their goals or results. Much has been written on the 80/20 rule of effective business relationships, and the most productive customer relationships come from a small number of those in the channel. While there are many reasons for this, one simple one is evaluating why partnerships make sense at the beginning of the process.

By conducting a short but effective opportunity analysis, some quantification is applied to the process. The starting point will be the business reasons that have caused the evaluation of the process in the first place. Why do I plan to do this? What value will be gained as a result? Most organizations now understand that it is not possible for them to do it all, and therefore some partnering is mandatory for the effective development of their business plan. Examples might be outsourced payroll, Websites, HR, procurement systems, and the like. These decisions are usually a little easier to make than strategic outsourcing of complex and mission critical business functions, such as Enterprise Resource Planning, sales and distribution, or supply chain applications. In these cases, a serious evaluation of where to go first, and why, needs to be conducted.

In the analysis several stages drive the requirements (see Table 10.1)

Table 10.1 Example of potential partnership opportunities to be considered.

Business need	Task to meet need	Profile of partner	Internal impact
Increase sales	Expand sales organization	Potential distributor with market knowledge	Build support mechanism to support partner
Build new product line	Development and manufacturing expansion	Outsourced design shop and manufacturing plant	Funding and management of the program

Once the basic opportunity has been identified, then detail needs to be added to determine whether this makes sense or not. In some cases, issues such as intellectual property or core competency will determine whether a partnership would ever make sense. For example, if an organization is concerned that there may be overlap with capabilities that are core to the firm, they may decide that this is so important to the business that it would never be outsourced. Software and high tech organizations are often concerned to ensure that they do not overlap or potentially compete with other partners, or they are very cautious about relicensing agreements to ensure that this is not a major problem for the future.

If the initial mapping of requirements and partners passes this first litmus test, then a more detailed analysis needs to be made of the potential partnership option. This would include:

» measuring the cost associated with the development of the relationship;
» determining the margin and cost of goods sold with the partnerships;
» re-engineering costs associated with the partner relationships;
» additional costs for marketing, sales, training, management, and maintenance of the relationship;
» if a distribution partnership, then agreement on metrics and goals for the sale of goods, and supporting costs.

At a high level this can be a simple ROI analysis, with the inputs and outputs of the partnership being measured. Sometimes partnerships still make sense, regardless of whether there are cost savings or measurable financial results. In some cases the development of a partnership is just inevitable, because there is no option but to deal with a particular firm or organization. This is usually where a firm is embedded in an existing supply chain or service that is key to the business operation, for example an e-commerce site without support for Visa or Mastercard would be a difficult sell, so not every relationship needs to go through the analysis, but the large ones should.

4. THE FRAMEWORK

After we have completed the POA and it appears that the next stages are on the cards, then the development of an internal framework to manage the partner process is recommended.

The development, implementation, and management of the partnership process have five basic stages. These are:

» planning
» research and preparation (R & P)
» implementing
» operation
» expansion.

A great deal of detail is contained in each of the steps, however the cycle is fairly straightforward. Planning begins with ensuring that the organization is ready for the change. This is not as simple as it sounds.

5. PLANNING

The CRO will work systematically through the stages to develop a "customer focused" strategy, while ensuring that the firm does not get sidetracked down paths inappropriate for their programs. A firm's readiness is the first stage in this process, and this immediately causes us start to run back into those earlier comments on values and vision. Both of these need to be aligned, but also the attitude needs to be right.

Readiness

Partnerships are based on a mysterious network of relationships and processes. Some businesses seem naturally good at choosing partners and partnering opportunities, and use their dominant position in an industry to best their competitors. Others struggle to deal with the control aspects of giving part of their business to another firm. Regardless of your perspective on partners and why they are important, the ability to attract, retain, and maintain effective partnerships will be the foundation of business in the future. Attitude and values become critically important in getting ready.

At the heart of partnership is conflict. Most of us want some control over the result of a project. Whether the task is simple, such as the development of a drawing or letter, or as complex as the development of a bridge, we want to control the outcome. While more organizations continue to work and rely on teams inside and outside the organization, many also wrestle with this reliance on others. To illustrate this point, just watch a child's soccer game. Kids playing soccer congratulate a teammate when they score the winning goal, or when their goalkeeper stops the other team's shot just before the end of the game. The reinforcement of their partnership as a team provides bonding. They are enjoying the upside of winning together. However, when things are not going so well, the praise turns rapidly to censure. Blaming others for not collecting the pass, missing the goal, all the time individuals getting ready to justify their position as a "contributor" to the team during the next bench time in the game. We rapidly return to our position of control, and defensiveness, rapidly diminishing the benefits from any earlier praise.

Attitude is just one aspect of measuring the readiness of staff to enter a partnership program. Many other elements need to be factored into the planning stages, including the measurement factors for the development of the program.

In order to build an effective plan, metrics need to be determined that will allow participants on all sides to understand what they are getting into and how the system will operate. This is often one of the most difficult elements for operations to deal with, as most companies know what they want out of it, but do not often understand that their partner also sees it the same way. This results in the all too often missed expectations and misunderstandings that cause partnerships to languish and fail. The communications systems that will support the program are almost the most important aspect of this process, as many failures occur in misunderstandings about deliverables and communication means in the organization.

Metrics and effectiveness

The metrics for partnership operation need to be clearly defined, for two reasons. Firstly the common understanding of both (or more) parties should understand what they are getting into and what the results should be, and secondly, metrics are needed to establish the effectiveness of the project. If the objective is to generate more business as a result of a partnership, then the key elements are what constitutes success, and who is responsible for it needs to be documented.

In all cases, the amount of documentation should be limited only to what is actually needed to achieve the goal, but commission payments, royalties, and other issues will fall by the wayside if they are not documented and calculated accordingly. This will lead to the inevitable misunderstandings that cause fractures in the relationship. Trust has to be developed in a relationship, but the results of trust have to be measured.

Each task associated with a potential strategy can be broken down into actionable items that will in turn be measured according to agreement. Table 10.2 illustrates some examples of the typical distribution agreement, and how metrics and results will be communicated.

Each of these metrics needs to be quantified by agreed processes and values that all parties agreed to in advance. The example above looks simple enough, however the devil is in the details. Ensuring that reporting schedule, individuals, methods, and processes are lined up is critical for the success of the operation at the implementation phase. All of these details do not have to be ironed out at this planning stage, but they do have to be recognized as issues that have to be addressed.

Program

Early identification of the elements in the program is an important planning stage. The essentials of the program, and how it is going to work have to be considered carefully at the planning stage. If there are

Table 10.2 Metrics and measurements for a partnership relationships.

Task	Metric	Communication channel
Sales from Partner A	Type of product, numbers of product, $ volume, discount elements, amount per month/quarter.	Partner sales management. Finance/order entry. Customer support for installation/ maintenance support. Defined protocols for all of the above.
Sales forecasts from Partner A	Estimates of new product sales, reported monthly, by product, region, salesperson. Sales pipeline report reflects the reporting stages and probability criteria agreed by both parties.	Input to sales department accepting forecasts from Partner A. Forecast reviewed with Partner A, then sent to manufacturing for advanced planning input.

barriers to making the program work then an evaluation of alternatives and what they are worth in the overall business scenario should be conducted. These can be as simple as considering whether something will work in a particular environment (for example a distribution agreement in an overseas market) through to major re-engineering and partnership program development for joint ventures such as building a new airplane. Factors that will affect the effectiveness and risk associated with a program become intimately tied to the financial and business issues driving the program.

Defining the program elements for less ambitious, but important partnerships can be outlined more systematically, with some good predictors of success. In the end, financial goals often become the long-term measure, even if an organization decides to take a phased approach, where the initial partnership strategy is primarily to gain market share, or extend distribution, these should ultimately have some bottom line impact for the operation.

In general greater work is required to scope out the inside and nearside partners than those in the business network. Because there are usually more of these in the overall business strategy, and the business is not necessarily relying on the success of one particular partner (which can be the case in an inside or nearside partnership).

Encourage

Enthusiasm is contagious. So is the lack of it. All planning stages must have an element of encouragement for the project included. This encouragement must be based on some tangible benefits for the participants. Members of the team will need to understand why they are involved in the process, what the benefits to them will be, and be fully supportive of corporate or other goals that will be specifically beneficial to them. Partnership programs that are starting out in existing environments (which most evolve from), often meet massive resistance. Depending on the reasons for starting the channel, encouragement can be easily built into the program, or can be a futile effort. Relationships have to be win-win for all involved, that includes staff as well as the business.

If you find that you have to do too much selling in your encouragement program this could be an early symptom of problems to come, for example:

» your staff do not believe the plan will work;
» the change required to make the program work has not been sufficiently discussed or worked out; and
» the staff are completely resistant to change regardless of the benefits.

Of all of these issues, the latter one is the most difficult to solve. In the past, many situations are made more difficult by natural resistance to change, and sometimes this can be fatal for new initiatives. (Note how many Web teams and start-ups from existing bricks-and-mortar firms have been funded as separate business units). This same principle also applies to channels programs.

Value proposition

The final element in the planning phase is the development of the value proposition. Some simple mathematics can assist in the development of this process. Every partnership has an impact on an existing business function. Sometimes it affects more than just one.

To develop the value proposition, some simple analysis of the cost associated with creating the new process and system is required.

The metrics from the planning process will provide the input for the development of the value proposition. By taking the input from each of these systems, it will be relatively easy to input these factors into the equation below, thereby beginning to provide input to the value proposition for the project or program.

$$\frac{\text{(New costs - Previous costs)} + \text{Development costs for program}}{\text{Number of units of measurement (sales, product, productivity)}}$$

The above metrics can often help to create the environment that will help the conversion to a CRO operation. However, sometimes it just makes sense to do it regardless of the evaluation mechanisms that are outlined here. For example, major change or a move into a new marketplace, can cause large variations, despite the costs, and sometimes without a short-term view on return on investment. Good examples of these transitions include core competency transitions in order to take advantage of new market opportunities. The telecommunications industry is a perfect example of this, particularly during the development of the Internet. The traditional bricks-and-mortar telecoms understood voice and how to leverage their network, but most did not comprehend the issues associated with data. Most of these firms went on massive core competency transitions to help them bring this capability in-house and fast. Buying sprees, education, and restructuring all made up part of the program. The point is that partnerships can help to complement and optimize a business operation, but are unlikely to change its core competency in a hurry.

The value proposition should provide the following guidelines as input to the next stages of the program (Table 10.3).

Table 10.3 Illustration of the measured impact of CRM and partnership strategies applied to existing processes.

Business function	Current process	Current cost	New process	Aggregate cost (y = new cost)
Sales	Direct	$x per unit (efficiency)	Indirect through partners	$x–y
Manufacturing	In-house, offshore plants	$x per unit	Through partners	$x–y
Marketing	Direct mail	$x per unit (lead)	e-marketing	$x–y
Support	Help desk with voice	$x per unit (per call)	Help desk with e-support functions	$x–y
Finance	Payroll	$x per unit (payroll)	Outsourced payroll though database firm	$x–y
Exchange	Not applicable	NA	Listing and membership on portal	$y

6. RESEARCH AND PREPARATION (R&P)

Before implementing a partnership program, some important elements need to be in place. Often partnership programs are not appropriately researched before the selection process begins. This usually results in the negative outcome of the 80/20 rule – signing up partners that will not get the job done. An ounce of prevention in this process can greatly improve results. Some of the most successful partnership programs that have been implemented still suffer from this problem, and companies seem strangely willing to continue to do business with partners that are not "cutting it." We would not continue to use a dentist we did not have confidence in, or select a homebuilder that seemed to ignore our needs, yet firms put up with partnerships that are not working effectively. Usually the most ineffective partnerships are the ones making the most noise about the companies' products, and have the best excuses as to why they cannot make their quota. Getting rid of partners is an important element in the overall management of a program, but the best way to avoid the task is do not do business with them in the first place.

Research

Most great partnerships start with some research at the beginning of the process. As the need for the project is identified during the planning stages, detailed input is provided for the research phase. Depending what business needs have been identified, profiles can be built for the type of partner being sought and potential partners then rated accordingly.

Research will also provide the list of potential partners that will be a good match for the company and the particular partnership needs of the project.

The factors that are likely to assist in this profiling will include:

» goals
» vision
» value matching (partner match with minimized conflict)
» culture
» communication
» skills
» technology compatibility
» market goals
» industry-specific experience
» partnership history
» process compatibly
» geographic location.

Identify

Once the list has been completed and the market testing is complete, the matching against individual firms can be conducted and concluded. Typical matching for partnership will consist of the following stages:

» review of the target firm;
» measurement of their skills, values, and organization against the partnership needs (potential test marketing of the program to test content of the system);

» ability to meet new work processes required for the system;
» support and business sustainability (will this be a long-term relationship); and
» geography and operational support.

Agreements

A lot of programs and partnerships fail around the agreement. In pre-Internet times, agreements could take months to complete (some still do), and blind-siding a partner by not providing a heads-up on the agreement requirements can cause major problems. Firms that have focused on joint venture and supply chain applications understand the importance of getting these ducks lined up early. Many firms still believe that their terms and conditions are the ones that have to be met, without any changes, under any circumstances. Only firms that have a near monopoly in an industry can exact such terms. For the rest of us it is important to assuage the pain to reach agreement.

Building legal agreements for e-business and partnerships can be a complex process, however. What you want to protect, measure, reward, and ultimately how to resolve disputes should all be contained in the agreement. Generally, distribution agreements are shorter and simpler than supply chain or joint development ventures. In many cases now the distribution agreements are available on-line, and in certain cases where firms sign up on-line for services, they can be self-service, sometimes only requiring a credit card and verification of services. Making it easy to sign up for services can dramatically increase the base. Recently, a B2B site in the construction industry signed up more than 3400 individuals from 200 companies in seven days from site launch. This is only achieved by making the legal agreement process simple and non-painful. Developing the requirements for the agreement in advance can dramatically increase the sign-up rate once the program is ready to be implemented. In the case of Web-based operations, particular care needs to be taken in these cases.

7. IMPLEMENTATION

The meat of the process is obviously in the implementation. Here many different elements have to be considered in order to achieve success in the entire process. Do not expect this to take a single pass. The management of relationships is a dynamic process.

Implementing the relationship is where the rubber meets the road. Now we are beyond the validation, and emphasis needs to be placed on making things work. Dealing with the apparatus of the partnership systematically dramatically reduces the risk and, probably most importantly, the timelines associated with generating results from the program.

Taking a proactive approach can create millions in value and reduce the timeframes to reaching revenue and savings. The more effort that is put in at these early stages, the greater the potential for success. One good starting point for the CRO implementation is the cultures that are going to operate in the partnership.

Culture

Culture has to be taken into account early in the implementation process. Dependent on the values and the method of operation inside the partnership, expectations and methods of doing business can vary radically.

Individuals want to thrive in operations that have integrity, trust, honesty, and other values that create the culture for the way they treat each other and, of course, their clients. Matching culture in partnerships is very important. There is nothing wrong with hiring staff that have a high performance and work patterns, but it can be a problem if they collide with other company-specific values. Matching and understanding these cultural differences during the course of developing a program is very important.

While it is not totally important that every relationship has a perfect match on all cultural fronts, one issue is critical in solving these problems: trust. Trust is the foundation of any relationship between any two operations. Once lost, it is very hard to retain, and months of effort can be wasted. Trust starts as a personal subject, but rapidly spreads through the organization once it takes hold. This has both a positive and negative impact, dependent on how things are going in the relationship.

While a perfect match is unlikely, understanding of values and culture will assist in the resolution of almost all other matters that affect the partnership.

In order to develop the relationship effectively early in the process, trying to build an understanding of the partner's needs is fundamental to success. This is not a selling issue; this is real relationship development. The box below contains a few suggestions for moving through this process. These are designed for the entire team, not just the lead on the project. Remember you have to ensure that cultural understanding and alignment are in place for the relationship. If this is not achieved early in the process friction will start early; finger pointing, excuses, failures, and no mechanism to solve the inevitable problems.

BEST PRACTICES FOR PARTNER ALIGNMENT

1 **Build shared agendas** comprising of shared goals, mechanisms, and involving all the team. Where there are problems, agree how they will be handled, by whom, and over what time period.
2 **Listen hard to each other**. Listening is often one of the hardest things to do at the beginning of a relationship. Remember you are not just selling each other, the relationship has to work beyond the development stage. Try and really understand and have empathy with the other partner's view and goals. Relay these to each other.
3 **Illustrate the values and culture of your operation**. In the early stages of a relationship create some examples of how you and the organization work. This will help with expectations. Even if some of these issues seem like a negative, ensure that the parties recognize this early in the process.
4 **Emphasize the goals**. One method that is very effective in the development of partnership strategies is focusing on the goals and benefits associated with the partnership. Having the metrics in place, and the value proposition clearly defined, organizations can be motivated to make behavior change occur.

Process

How to do it? The processes that make up the relationship and how the relationship is going to operate are a fundamental basis for implementing success. This is never more important than in the development of e-business and self-service applications. In these scenarios many firms have difficulty in understanding how the process works, mainly because most of the action occurs electronically. For many organizations using exchanges or procurement sites for the first time, it is very difficult for operations to understand what the process looks like. The stages, rules, and processes for each of the applications can be dealt with differently.

Determining how new processes will look will be based on a number of factors. These include:

» policies and procedures;
» work practices between the various groups involved;
» integrity of the business transaction; and
» speed and business objectives from the process.

Particularly when developing e-business processes, the need is to minimize the amount of human interaction inside the business processes. E-business has an insatiable appetite to replicate and reduce the number of human "hand-offs." One of the major reasons that the Internet has been so scalable in the development of business systems has been due to the "process optimization." Well-established organizations like Dell have streamlined the ordering process by externalizing their configuration management software, allowing users to build their own systems to order. By integrating their back office system, they have dramatically improved the efficiency of their systems. It also becomes easy to provide feedback for the user, giving them further options that they might find useful, and of course the configuration manager will only allow the customer to order things that can be built.

While there is much efficiency for both the vendor and the customer in the Internet model, there are some advantages to the manual process. Physical interaction with sales staff to discuss and comprehend the options is still more effective face-to-face. However, as more of these transactions become "commodity" in nature, the advantages start to wane. Hence it is now almost impossible to purchase many non-mainstream products through main street or mall stores today, so great is the advantage of the e-business model from the vendor's perspective.

Organizations use many models to assist them in the development of new business processes. In the development of partnerships, the business goals of the partnership will be the primary guidance for the development of new systems. Workshops, seminars, and the documentation of existing processes are good mechanisms to assist in the development of the new systems. Savings should be looked for in the following areas:

» time to complete a process;
» number of processes;
» performing tasks electronically where possible;
» cutting the number of parties involved in a process;
» allowing electronic tools and processes to assist in the purchasing and negotiation process.

Using either internal or external facilitators can assist in the development of new processes, and improve the timeliness of the solutions. External facilitators can have an advantage if you are negotiating and developing new processes that have internal and external partners involved.

8. CUSTOMER RELATIONSHIP MANAGEMENT (CRM)

The Customer Relationship Management (CRM) element of a system is a major concern for any partnership program. Partnerships require management of information about clients, prospects, partners, and others that are included in the company's business network.

> CRM – Customer Relationship Management systems improve and optimize methods of managing the interface and interaction with existing and prospective clients.

The CRM is usually based on a relational database system with differing views of the database according to the needs and application of the users. Although the technology is now referred to as a CRM, the partnership application management can be based on the same structure.

The CRM is a tremendous boom for the development of a CRO strategy. Chosen and implemented carefully, the system will provide the framework to help create, manage, and exploit a partnership system. Critical functions that are managed with the CRM include:

» customer and partner contact information; and
» relationship data including:
  » sales
  » marketing
  » finance
  » support
  » operations.

Specific applications related to the above can be built that will allow the population and management of these systems. For example, firms like Amazon and others will allow individuals to enter information inside large CRMs that track the characteristics of how the individual or firm operates. As a result they can determine, though the combined use of e-marketing and CRM systems, how a prospect is using their system, and this allows them to make one-to-one offerings.

The ability to be able to customize the experience for the user is a critical element for success in the implementation of these systems. As most businesses have a wide range of contacts within their scope, effectively leveraging and managing this pool is of great importance to their ability to partner effectively. Just take the numbers of contacts that even the smallest organization makes over the course of a year. Aside from existing customers, there are prospects, leads from trade shows, professional contacts, and personal contacts. How many of these are pooled into a central base where they can be leveraged for further use? E-marketing campaigns and other traditional means are often co-ordinated in a manner that will not leverage these relationships over the long haul.

At the most basic level the CRM is the repository of information to start this process. After all, we cannot market or manage the information if we have no way of even seeing what is happening at the contact level. Most organizations now understand the value of this data, and that it needs to be the starting point of any successful partner or client relationship system.

9. THE KNOWLEDGE MANAGEMENT SYSTEM (KM)

The Knowledge Management System is another great lever in the cause to better service partners and clients from e-business systems. In

Chapter 3 the importance of KM was emphasized with good reason. Unless we capture the best practices, the data about the way we want others to understand our product and services, it is impossible for them to operate more efficiently.

> "Knowledge Management: The leverage and optimization of information inside an organization to improve quality, responsiveness, processes, and timeliness of relevant information transfer."

Quietly but steadily, the KM strategy for organizations has become increasingly important. Although KM has not been the most exciting initiative for many, it is one that creates huge value to organizations that embrace it fully. Whether you are planning to leverage the knowledge of existing staff more effectively or improve the productivity of others, KM can help. For partnerships, KM becomes a prerequisite, particularly if e-business partnerships are needed.

In e-business, partners want immediate access to the most relevant information about a product or service. This could be a revised maintenance procedure, or a simple product description. If the information has not been made available to the organization, then there is no way that you can leverage it. Development of KM strategies has been the topic of many books, seminars, and consulting initiatives. Not as glamorous as other cousins important to successful e-business partnerships, it nevertheless remains a foundation class.

Like many other technologies, the KM class is of little use without the accompanying best practices and processes. In fact, most of the benefits used in the development and deployment of these systems lie in the integrated nature of the actual rollout. These systems require changes in the way that information is gathered, distributed, and re-used throughout the operation. Externalizing it to partners is a logical next stage in the optimization of the system. Most KM systems comprise of the following technology components:

» intranets;
» document repositories;
» existing paper based systems (filing, etc.);
» electronic filing systems (electronic imaging technologies);
» workflow products;
» electronic storage systems.

For the purposes of the technology discussion, the back office systems are separated from the KM system. In reality these often form the backbone of many partner strategies and e-business portals. However, as much of the information that comprises of a KM system is spread around the operation, capturing and manipulating it in an intelligent form usually becomes the foundation of the organization's KM strategy.

Knowledge Management combined with CRM technologies can provide at least a factor of 10 times improvement in results when the implementations are linked. In my own experience, the CRM systems are much less valuable if they are not tied to the data that will assist in the resolution of problems once the partner has connected with the system. For example, a partner logs into their support Website. They log on to a password-protected portion of the site, permitting access to a privileged area of your system that has been specifically created to ensure access to information relevant for their partnership. Immediately, the partner is looking for support information regarding a new product, perhaps references or documentation of a client's experience with the product. Unless the partner is given access to the relevant knowledge base where this data resides, they will need to call and use the "old network" method of getting the right information. Knowing who holds this data and how best to extract it from them can be a challenge for internal staff in an organization – it may take months for your partners to figure this "network" out for themselves. Far better to offer this information in electronic form, then the partner can "serve themselves" the information, cutting your costs and their costs and improving their client satisfaction. The KM system will provide the adhesive that links partner information with the data they are looking for, closing the loop on the experience.

A tremendous by-product of this process is that once in place, these systems scale. By merely adding more computing and storage power to their network that contains the information, many more partners and their clients can be served the information they are looking for, with virtually no impact on the headcount and staffing levels inside your own organization. Similar to the comments made by many a software executive, it is creating the first good version that is expensive; once in place, the operating costs to re-use the same data are relatively low.

Make Knowledge Management an area that is high on your list of first stopping points in the development of the partnership strategy. The rewards are very high for those that want to invest early in the process.

Knowledge management strategies have created huge value for operations such as Cisco Systems. Capturing and disseminating the relevant information to their partner network has created huge savings made in quality information transfer. This has resulted in many self-service applications that allow their partners access to the appropriate and relevant information in seconds, without any direct staff interaction. This type of improvement can only be made by externalizing an internal KM strategy as a foundation.

10. BACK OFFICE

The back office today represents a very wide range of technologies that are central to the success of e-business solutions. The ones most discussed are often in the manufacturing and development industries. Enterprise Resource Planning systems and their accompanying products have been the subject of major investment for engineering-based firms in recent years. The successes and failures have been well documented.

However, back office is not limited to ERP systems or their derivatives. These could be trading systems for finance operations, control systems for utilities, distribution systems for shippers; the lists go on. Every firm has some core back office technology systems that are tightly bound to the way that the operation does business. These are the systems without which their businesses would be unable to operate. Many of these systems are legacy systems that have been in place for a long time and were often implemented with a view to internal use, not external partnerships. For the larger operations that viewed partnerships in terms of "you are my partner" – which translated to "I own you, and you will play by my rules if you are in my supply chain" – these systems could turn out to be a liability.

In order to leverage the information contained in these systems the technology has to be applied to allow previously closed systems to become open, fixed procedures to become flexible, my business rules to start to reflect *our* business rules.

Billions of dollars have been and continue to be spent on the resolution of these problems. Partnership systems cannot be created if people cannot track orders, view inventory status, place orders, view delivery times, and control configuration options. The insight into the operation has to become seamless with the overall goals of the partnership, and this can only be done by externalizing the back offices systems appropriately. Many of the e-commerce problems with delivery over the holiday shopping periods have been a direct result of these issues. Although the consumer appeared to be ordering products in time, the back office integration required to provide the visibility regarding inventory, delivery, and availability was not in place. The result was chaos and a great lack of consumer confidence in the marketplace. Business-to-business systems need this integration to even a greater extent; as the process becomes more seamless, so the value in the partnerships increases. Integration of the business processes and the back office systems blaze the trail for advances in partnerships.

Back office systems can comprise many different sub-systems and processes. The primary ones included in partnership systems are:

» financial
» manufacturing
» inventory
» advanced planning
» business intelligence
» decision support systems
» configuration management
» Enterprise Resource Planning
» supply chain software
» internal business exchanges.

Back office will always be involved in any CRM situation, regardless of the scale and scope of the relationship. The more broadly based the requirements, the greater the level of back office integration. It also follows that the efficiency of the overall process improves as does the depth of back office integration. Due to the nature of the expense associated with changing back office systems, organizations are often loath to make extensive changes without extremely careful examination of the repercussions.

Frequently Asked Questions (FAQs)

Q1: What is CRM?

A: See Chapter 1.

Q2: What are the world's most valuable CRM programs?

A: Chapter 5 illustrates the market size, and how firms are making CRM critical to their success.

Q3: Who is responsible for CRM development within an organization?

A: Details of who and how CRM programs can be built are outlined in Chapter 10.

Q4: I want to create and develop a CRM system. How do I go about it?

A: See Chapter 10.

Q5: What does the term "CRM" mean, and why is it important?

A: See Chapter 2.

Q6: How have others created value from their CRM programs?

A: See Chapter 7 for examples of where organizations show how CRM programs have helped these operations.

Q7: What are the best practices of others to improve the way that CRM operates?

A: Best practices of leading CRM practitioners are outlined in Chapter 7.

Q8: What are good real-world examples of successful CRM operations?

A: How Ceridian Canada, Bose and Singapore Cable Vision have made successful operations are outlined in Chapter 7.

Q9: How do I find out more about the subject?

A: Details of additional resources for CRM are in Chapter 9.

Q10: What are the origins of CRM?

A: Chapter 3 has all the info on the development of CRM.

Index

Printed and bound in the UK by
CPI Antony Rowe, Eastbourne

Printed and bound by CPI Group (UK) Ltd, Croydon, CR0 4YY

13/04/2025

14656562-0001